HONOLULU COP

Reflections on a Career with HPD

Gary A. Dias

THE
BESS
PRESS

3565 Harding Ave. Honolulu, Hawai'i 96816
808/ 734-7159   www.besspress.com

Design: Carol Colbath

Library of Congress Cataloging-in-Publication Data

Dias, Gary A.
  Honolulu cop : reflections on a career
with HPD / Gary A. Dias.
     p.   cm.
  Includes illustrations.
  ISBN 1-57306-146-8
  1. Dias, Gary A. 2. Police - Hawaii -
Honolulu - Biography. 3. Honolulu. Police
Dept. - History. I. Title.
HV7911.D52.A33 2002   363.2-dc21

Printed in the United States of America

For Ryan, Kevin, Samantha, and Alexis

and

the men and women of the
Honolulu Police Department
…who truly have
the toughest, dirtiest, most satisfying job in town

Contents

Acknowledgments

Putting words to paper was the easy part of this book. All I needed do was write out the memories. Reviewing the manuscript, trying to catch errors, and suggesting improvements required the skill of a professional writer. For that I am sincerely grateful to my wife Robbie Dingeman, who spent many patient hours at the computer reviewing this work.

A note of thanks is also owed to the Honolulu Police Department, Tom Hisamura of the City and County of Honolulu, and The Queen's Medical Center for assistance in locating and permission to use the photos in this book.

Photo Credits
The photos on pages 17, 63, 73, 128, and 129 are by Robbie Dingeman. All other photos are used with permission of the Honolulu Police Department.

What it's all about.

Preface

This book was thirty years in the making. I entered the Honolulu Police Department (HPD) in 1971 and retired in 1998. The years in between were packed full of events, some funny, some sad, some scary.

Over the years, I saw assignments on foot; motorized on the Windward coast; on the receiving desk, with Honolulu District One Patrol; and in the Criminal Investigation Division, Internal Affairs, the Communications Division, the Scientific Investigation Section, Informational Resources, and the Traffic Division. I grew through the years from a lowly foot patrol officer—the way we all began—to the rank of major at the time of my retirement.

I had the fortunate and exciting opportunity to head HPD's Homicide Detail for six challenging years and to be in charge of its Hostage Negotiation Team during that same time. I was lucky to attend, in 1987, seminars in homicide investigations with the FBI and the New York State Police, the latter an agency for which I have the utmost respect. I also attended advanced crime scene training the following year, again at both locations. I got to meet and speak with investigators who tackled some of our nation's most horrific crimes, such as former FBI Agent John Douglas, a founder of the FBI's elite Serial Killing and Sexual Homicide Profiling Team.

Perhaps more important in later years was seeing firsthand how other agencies conducted their investigations. Through observing their values and their departmental cultures, I realized just how different we were in Honolulu.

Our department in Honolulu seemed much more a part of the community than was the case with many of our mainland counterparts. Discussions with other homicide commanders left me with the impression that their relationships with their communities were cold, without a feeling of belonging. They were outsiders—coming in, doing their jobs, and leaving again.

HPD may have been a few years behind mainland departments in terms of technology, but we were, and continue to be, leaders in the field of community relationships. Perhaps it's because we are an island state. Perhaps it's because so many people are related to so many other people and are friends of so many others as well. The concept of *six degrees of separation* is alive and doing very well in Honolulu. People frequently asked me, "You related to the Diases in Waimānalo?" "You related to the Diases in Wai'anae?" Even the "new" community policing concept introduced to Honolulu by Chief Michael Nakamura in the early nineties really wasn't new. We were doing community policing in the seventies.

Sadly, to quote Bob Dylan, "The times, they are a-changing." The past thirty years have seen our community move further and further away from having beat cops who know the people on their beats. Our population has grown. Our department has grown. And I'm not sure how successful our department will be in maintaining the type of policing that Honolulu once knew.

Perhaps one of the ways to do this is by teaching our kids and our communities that the police are a part of, not apart from the community, to paraphrase Sir Robert Peel. Peel's reform of the London Metropolitan Police over 170 years ago transformed the role of the police in their communities. He emphasized service, not force. He emphasized that police need the willing cooperation of law-abiding communities. Peel also emphasized that the police must maintain a complete impartiality toward the law along with a complete impartiality toward the public in administering the law.

I really enjoy teaching. I learned this when I was asked to instruct recruit classes on crime-scene investigation. I later obtained my master's degree in criminal justice administration and became a board certified forensic examiner with the American College of Forensic Examiners. I continue teaching at the University of Hawai'i–West O'ahu, Chaminade University of Honolulu, and Wayland Baptist University. I use many of my law enforcement experiences to emphasize points of instruction, and I have heard so many times from students, "You ought to write a book."

So I did. In this book, by telling about some funny, sad, and scary events that occurred through the years, I relate what it was like—from my perspective—to be a police officer in Honolulu during the last thirty years of the twentieth century.

I certainly do not remember verbatim conversations held thirty years ago. But the conversations and events that appear in the following pages represent my memory of how they went, and the feeling that remained because of them. In the retellings, I have disguised the identities of the not-so-innocent and of my *cumpades* who joined me in a few foolish episodes over the years.

Every now and then I add my opinions and my personal comments. In discussing some of the frailties of our department, I do so with the knowledge that no police department is perfect. But a good department learns from its mistakes, just as good officers learn from their mistakes. The men and women of the Honolulu Police Department are among our nation's best, who learn from their mistakes and try to provide top quality service to our community.

And in that regard, you absolutely won't find two currently retired police officers pouring gasoline into a planter box ever again.

1971 HPD recruitment poster

1
On Entering the Police Profession

Why in the world would anyone want to join a police force? Especially in the early seventies. Especially when it would mean a drop in pay. That was one of the questions they asked in the HPD employment interview: "Why do you want to join the police department?" That's a tough one.

I started to think about becoming a police officer during high school. I think it was the image of the cop in uniform and the authority he represented. No, to tell the truth, it was the power he represented. Every so often you hear that HPD is "the toughest gang in town." Yeah, that was it. Being a police officer meant having the power to do things. What things? Carry a gun. Wear the uniform. Issue tags. Excitement every day on the job. What an image! Little did I know that the reality was something quite different. It took but a few years and an assignment to District Four, Kāne'ohe, to learn that the way I dealt with people was much more important than the tough-guy image I had created. Yet the image—positive or negative—of a police officer is so important for the public that it plays a big role in day-to-day police life.

My desire to become a police officer had to take a secondary role in 1968, however, as my foremost priority was getting a college degree. But in 1971 I found myself at a University of Hawai'i job fair, sitting with Sergeant Clyde Springer and listening to all the possibilities that awaited me at HPD. I remember the catchy advertising slogan HPD used: It's the toughest, dirtiest, most satisfying job in town. Never mind that I was a mere semester away from graduating, that cop job was there right now. I had spent three years watching many of my friends join the force while I continued to take sociology courses at the Mānoa campus. Well, enough was enough. I took the civil service exam and soon began a series of other prehiring requirements: a physical agility test, a medical exam, and a job interview.

Back then the physical agility test consisted of one, yes, one pull up, a sprint down a basketball court and back, a standing long jump, and something right out of a carnival sideshow: I had to squeeze a device that measured my hand strength. The medical exam was little more than a visit with a doctor, a TB test, and a urinalysis. The interview, however, was more challenging.

"Why do you want to become a police officer?"

I could feel the perspiration forming on my forehead. (I sweat easily under pressure.) So how does a twenty-year-old with very little life experience respond to that question? What type of person are they looking for? What would be an appropriate answer? I went back to my sociology background at UH.

"I want to help people?" I asked in response, hoping for a nod of the head or some other sign that my answer was the right one. The middle-aged part-Hawaiian officer glanced at me with eyes that said, *Yeah, sure.* He then went into a series of other not-so-difficult questions and I started to relax a little. "Can you work any shift? Can you work on weekends, Sundays, and holidays? Is transportation a problem? Will you uphold our laws?"

I was starting to feel confident, my sweating stopped, and I thought the interview was going rather well until he asked *the question.* When I had asked friends in the department about the hiring process—what did I need to know, what did I need to be on the lookout for—the majority of them said to watch for *the question.* They told me how they answered and what they thought the interviewer was looking for. But no one really knew what the correct answer was. Or even if there was a correct answer. Only one of my police officer friends claimed that the interviewer did not ask him *the question.* He didn't have any thoughts on a correct answer either.

The question was, "If your mother was speeding, would you tag her? Would you tag your mother?" My interviewer had a serious face but his eyes revealed a maniacal mind.

Beads of perspiration popped out on my forehead. I could feel the sweat rolling down my stomach inside my shirt. *Jesus! Of course I wouldn't tag my mother. What kind of stupid question was that?* I started to think I'd finish my degree at UH after all. I wouldn't take the test for the Fire Department—I couldn't handle heights. Yup, UH would be fine.

"No, I wouldn't tag my mother," I said truthfully, but dejectedly, sure that it was not the answer he wanted.

"What would you do? Just let her speed off? After all, you're the police officer. What would you do?"

I felt certain now that my answer was wrong. His follow-up question indicated to me that he would have tagged *his* mom. What a guy.

"I would tell her to quit embarrassing me."

He gave me that look again: a stare that told me his brain was working, but gave me no clue to his thoughts. The interview ended a few minutes later, and I went home feeling like a complete failure. I also puzzled over the possibility that a police officer was expected to tag his mom. I warned my mom: if I ever got into the police department, she was never to speed in front of me. In a few weeks, I started to perk up. Besides, it was time to register again for UH and I had to concentrate on the courses I needed. (It would actually be more than twenty years before I completed that degree and then obtained my master's degree in criminal justice administration.)

Mrs. Edna Jones called a couple of days before I was supposed to register and informed me that I was accepted to the fifty-fourth recruit class of the Honolulu Police Department. What UH courses? I was ecstatic. I was on my way. To less money, to long hours, to long stretches of boredom—to becoming the police officer I wanted to be.

2
Recruit School

"Recruit school" really was a misnomer. There was no school. Just two classrooms at the old police station at Pawaʻa Annex. (The old station actually was a renovated Sears.) There was no police academy then either. Recruit school was run by the Training Division. The HPD Police Academy would come many years later. Recruit training consisted of classes on the penal code, policies, rules, and procedures taught by seasoned police officers. There was Sergeant Springer again. He was our recruit sergeant, the person responsible for our class, the fifty-fourth recruit class.

I was hired on June 16, 1971, but class didn't start for two weeks. Personnel Division needed the additional time to complete the hiring. Those of us who had already been hired were temporarily assigned to various divisions to do odd jobs until the class was convened. I was assigned to the Records Division along with several other new recruits. Our job was to transport old reports from the records office and file them in the basement storage room. It was tedious, but we did get an interesting surprise when we discovered a box of old homicide reports, including black-and-white photos of the scenes and victims.

There were two classrooms at the old station, and the fifty-third recruit class was already in progress. We tried to talk to those recruits when time permitted, to get an idea of what class was like. One recruit named Mike warned us to be wary of the old Japanese officer assigned to the Records Division. Mike was assigned there when he was hired, just as we were, and had a run-in with the old guy. That senior officer, named Kenji, was complaining about a stomachache. Mike had some Alka Seltzer with him and kindly offered two tablets to Kenji, who took the medicine with some reservation and left the room. A few minutes later, Kenji burst back into the office, bubbles coming from his nose and mouth and swearing, "You f—kirg haole, you try kill me." Mike said he leapt over a desk to escape the raging old man and ran around the room until a sergeant got between them. It was then that he learned that Kenji had never had Alka Seltzer before and tried to swallow the tablets with a glass of water, like aspirin. The story explained why Kenji was so rude to us.

Class finally started. The dress code was black or dark blue pants and a white shirt with a black tie. The haircut was short. Facial hair was not allowed during recruit school. We addressed everyone as "Sir." The course offerings were not difficult—at least no more difficult than senior year in high school. We were required to keep a journal that the instructors would judge at the end of the four-month

The first day of school for the fifty-fourth recruit class. The author is in the second row, third from the right.

process, and we had to pass every course. But the important thing was not the course content. It was the socialization process.

It was at recruit school that we learned to *become* police officers. We learned the language of police officers. We learned the shared culture, the shared values, the shared beliefs of police officers. It was through this process that we were drawn into the subculture known as law enforcement.

The early seventies brought a major recruiting push, of which my class was a part. The department was growing quickly to keep up with the population growth. This growth was also bringing an inner change as well. HPD was changing from a small-town department to a big-city department, with all the attendant problems. Perhaps the biggest change over the years was from a close-knit organization in which an individual officer knew all the other officers on the force and many of the people and businesses on his beat to a more distant association based on the formal relationship of anonymous police officer and community member.

The not-so-obvious result of this major recruitment drive was that from 1995 through the early 2000s, many police officers would retire. Another was that with the influx of patrol officers, promotions or assignments in divisions outside patrol were few. A greater percentage of officers would find themselves caught in the patrol assignment for many, many years.

Salary was an issue, too. Police officers were among the lowest-paid city employees. I left a job as a stock clerk at GEM Kapalama to join the police department and took a $300-a-month pay cut. Our paychecks were ridiculous. In addition to taxes, medical insurance, retirement, and post-retirement deductions, we had to pay Honolulu Police Relief Association (HPRA) dues and part of the cost of our uniforms. What was left was terribly little to live on and not enough to support a family for those who were married. Most of us lived at home by need rather than by choice.

The youngest recruits in our class were in their twenties; the oldest was in his forties. We came from very different backgrounds.

Many of us grew up on Oʻahu, two guys were from Maui, one was from the Big Island, and more than a few were from the mainland. One had recently returned from a tour in Vietnam. His recent military experience and his demeanor made him the prime candidate to be our class president. He was, surprisingly, the first of our class to leave the department. His experiences in the Vietnam War proved so traumatic that he would not load ammunition into his revolver. For a few months after recruit school, no one knew this. Then one day he announced that he was resigning because he knew he could not use his weapon against another human being. That belief forced him to carry an unloaded gun, and he knew he might endanger another officer who needed him in a firefight.

The years after recruit school saw our class dwindle. Several class members realized that the job was not for them and moved on. The two Maui guys transferred to the Maui Police Department, a couple of others were caught committing crimes against the law they swore to uphold, and two died of natural causes. The most tragic loss occurred when one of our classmates, for reasons unknown to me, shot and killed his wife, then killed himself. By the time I retired, only a few senior officers were from the fifty-fourth recruit class.

Recruit school, however, was a time we savored. Two of the most exciting times were getting first our uniforms and later our revolvers. The uniforms were issued first, because we needed them to train in public, on the street, directing traffic and operating traffic lights. We trained at the intersections of King Street and Kalākaua Avenue and King and Keʻeaumoku streets. (I would like now, after thirty years, to offer my apologies to those motorists who endured our quick light changes and the long delays while we decided that the traffic in the opposite direction needed a turn.) Everyone could tell we were recruits, not only by the number of us taking turns screwing up traffic, but also by the fact that we had no badges and no guns. We wouldn't get our badges until we graduated, and we couldn't carry a gun until we completed weapons training.

Most of us had not fired a weapon in our lives, and now we were going to carry one as if it had become part of us. We were sent to the police range at Koko Head Crater to get our weapons and begin training. As if it were a message that human life is so very fragile, on the way to class the first day we came upon a head-on collision on Kalaniana'ole Highway near Hanauma Bay. A woman in a car in the eastbound lane was killed. We tried to help, but there she was, dead in our arms. And there we were—going to a class to learn how to kill someone if we had to.

The process of learning about our weapons involved several things that I never understood. The instructors reveled in making us jog around the firing range parking lot while we smoked cheap cigars. We had to jog until our cigars were smoked down to two inches. Then we had to endure running through tear gas as we gasped for breath after the smoke-filled jog. The whole time, the instructors shouted insults and threatened to fire us if we weren't fast enough. I

Koko Head pistol range, circa 1970

began to wonder if this is what boot camp is like. (I was never in the service.)

Now that our lung capacity was sufficiently reduced and our pride destroyed, we finally began to learn about our guns and holsters: how to safely draw the weapon, how to hold it, how to aim it, how to dismantle it, how to clean it. *Enough already, let's go shoot it!* While we sat at the pistol range under the roof, the fifty-third recruit class was already ahead of us, practicing at the outdoor range. We could hear their bullets exploding as they fired at their targets. Jealous, we wished to join them. But then the shooting stopped and instructors sprinted to the field range, where one recruit had shot himself in the leg trying to quick-draw his weapon. The siren of the ambulance contrasted with the silence among our group. *You can get hurt doing this. It's not a game.*

In spite of all the sobering things that happened during the first few days of firearms training, we did succeed with our weapons. We learned how to quick-draw, fire six rounds into the target in a few seconds, reload, and do it again. We fired at the "suspect" target from a few yards away, from twenty-five yards, and from fifty yards. We fired during the day, and we fired at night. We fired the shotgun at clay birds, and we fired the AR-15 semiautomatic rifle with a scope. The firearms training not only familiarized us with our weapons, but also socialized us much more quickly into the roles of police officers.

We also participated in water safety and judo classes. You may think that on an island everyone knows how to swim. Not so. We had a quick lesson in water rescue. Fully clothed. Shoes and all. After all, if we were on the beat and someone needed to be rescued from a pool or beach, we couldn't very well say, "Excuse me while I put my gun and holster into the trunk and change into my shorts—be right back." So we trained—nearly drowned would be more accurate— while fully clothed at the Mānoa pool. Then one of the instructors got the bright idea that we should go to Waikīkī and swim the shoreline from one end to the other. Thank you, Sergeant Springer.

The water training wasn't half as bad as the judo training, which was part discipline, part self-defense. We spent several weeks in the dojo (a large room next to the radio shop, across the street from the station). The scary part was that most of the people training us were elderly Japanese men—a retired guy, a postal worker, and others who donated their time to helping HPD train—along with a couple of really big police officers, and each of them could, and did, kick our butts all around the dojo. A couple of us suffered only minor injuries until Harold proved that bending his elbow in the direction it's not meant to go was a bad thing to do.

One incident in particular stands out—the day Larry challenged Leo, one of the instructors. Leo was a former police officer who lost an eye responding to a bar fight. He left the department and went on to work for a local union. Leo was a large man. A very large man. Leo was a strong man. Very strong. Larry was skinny. Larry was selected by Leo to help demonstrate a submission technique known, in those days, as the *choke hold*. It's not called the choke hold anymore. That

HPD dojo, circa 1970

term is an attorney's dream in a civil suit. It's now called a *judo sub-mission hold.*

So there's Larry kneeling on the mat, with Leo kneeling behind him explaining the choke hold. First you place your strong arm around the suspect's neck so that the bend in your elbow is in front of his throat. You won't hurt the windpipe that way. Then you tighten your arm so that, simultaneously, the forearm presses against one side of the neck and the biceps press against the other. The hand of your weak arm pushes the back of the suspect's head forward, and the hand of your strong arm grabs your judo gi, or shirt, for support. While doing this, you pull or move backward to keep the suspect off balance. The technique is designed to reduce the flow of blood to the brain, causing the suspect to pass out within a few seconds. (Don't try this on anyone; people have died from this hold.)

Leo made the mistake of saying that when the choke hold is properly applied, the suspect cannot get free. Larry apparently considered that a challenge. He swiftly jerked free of Leo's loose grip on him, spun around Leo and applied his own version of the choke hold to Leo's very large neck. Leo calmly stood up, with Larry still hanging onto his neck. In what seemed like a fraction of a second, Leo reached over his shoulder, pulled Larry over his head, and spun him around to face him. Then, in what can only be described as pure beauty in motion, he fell backward, pulling Larry with him. As he reached the ground, he curled up and placed his feet on Larry's chest. Then he kicked upward. Larry hit the ceiling with a fairly loud *bang* and bounced at least twice on the mat. Larry didn't move after that landing, and I thought Leo had killed him. But the big man calmly sat Larry up and slapped his back a few times as we sat there blinking. Larry jerked to life, and Leo thanked him for being such a good assistant.

No one volunteered much during the remaining weeks of recruit school.

Today, our recruit academy offers a course of instruction equivalent to a college curriculum. In addition to offering the courses

The Police Recruit Academy: Ke Kula Makaiʻi

taught in 1971, HPD trains its recruits in self-defense, defensive driving, and pursuit driving, to name a few areas. An important aspect of recruit school is the mock-crime training. The academy uses a building with rooms that depict various scenes: a small business, a bedroom, a kitchen, an office. In these rooms, volunteers from the community play the roles of victims, suspects, and witnesses, and provide realistic scenarios that give the recruits an opportunity to respond as they would in the community. If a recruit fails here, he's washed out. Instructors provide recruits with as much assistance as possible, but it's better to lose a recruit during training than risk harm to people in our community.

Last I heard, cigars were not part of the firearms training.

3
Fourth Watch

I solemnly swear that I will faithfully support the Constitution and Laws of the United States of America and the Constitution and Laws of the State of Hawai'i, and that I will conscientiously and impartially discharge my duties as a Police Officer in the Police Department of the City and County of Honolulu, State of Hawai'i, and any and all other duties devolving upon me in connection with such office. So help me God.

With those words, the officers of the fifty-fourth recruit class entered the world of law enforcement—Hawai'i style. I don't remember the menu at the Coral Ballroom, but lunch was served, and our families were proud of us. I do remember that I felt awkward eating while in uniform, gun and all. Somehow, eating didn't seem appropriate for the uniform. Our graduation photo shows thirty-nine faces, looking rather grim and pensive. Only three guys were smiling. In spite of our police uniforms, the rest of us looked like suspects in a rogues' gallery of serial killers.

And that's what's inherently wrong with the image of police officers. We look too damn serious. And sometimes we take ourselves too damn seriously, too. When Michael Nakamura became chief of police, his smiling face and relaxed and friendly manner worked to break down the image of the stoic and impassive beat cop.

At the end of recruit school, with our graduation certificates in hand, we were all headed in the same direction—to the Fourth Watch. Each shift in a 24-hour period was known as a *watch*. First Watch—the graveyard shift—began at 2230 (10:30 p.m.) and ended

Graduation ceremonies for the fifty-fourth recruit class

at 0715 (7:15 a.m.). Second Watch, or the day shift, began at 0630 and ended at 1515, and the Third Watch, otherwise known as the swing shift, began at 1430 and ended at 2315. To further complicate matters, each watch had an alphabetical designation, A-Alpha, B-Bravo, or C-Charlie, that identified each group of officers as a separate, cohesive unit. Those on, say, Charlie Watch, automatically felt that Charlie Watch was better than Alpha and Bravo watches, and likewise for the other two watches.

The Fourth Watch (also known as Delta Watch), consisted of the just-graduated recruits. The shift ran from 1800 to 0215. To some, it was a great time. To others, it was pure hell. Fourth Watch consisted entirely of foot beats. About half of the beats were in downtown Honolulu and the other half were in Waikīkī. From our conversations with more senior officers and guys from the previous Fourth Watch, we learned that the choice beats were in Waikīkī. Life simply was better there than downtown, where drunks, drugs, and demimondaines (prostitutes) rule the night. We also learned that the worst beat of all was Beat One. It was located smack dab in the middle of Mayor Wright Housing, just far enough from downtown proper to give us the feeling that we were absolutely all alone in the middle of what may have been the toughest housing project on Oʻahu.

The Fourth Watch, at that time in 1971, was run primarily by three sergeants, Mike Joy, Frank Sua (both now deceased), and John Piper, who swapped off between downtown and Waikīkī. They were three of the most respected men the department has ever had in its ranks. They were the models we patterned ourselves after. Many of us wished to be officers just like Mike, Frank, and John.

Everyone was early the first day we reported to Fourth Watch. We gathered in the squad room, our uniforms crisp, our leather brilliant, and our hearts pounding. No more school. This was the real thing.

"Line up!" came the shout from Frank Sua, and we quickly formed several ranks, just as we had been taught.

" 'Ten-hut!" And we snapped to attention. The sergeants slowly walked the ranks, searching for something out of place. They took us through the drills that presented our weapons, handcuffs, flashlights, and batons for inspection and the formal drill procedures we would perform three times a week from that day on. After inspection we sat and listened to in-service training and lectures from the sergeants as to their expectations and what we could count on when we hit the road. But we were getting anxious to get out on the road and be *cops*. And then it came, our first assignment.

"Beat One: Dias."

"Sir!" I answered aloud. *Shit,* I thought. *Just my luck. Just my damned luck.*

We gathered at the Young Street entrance to the police department, and the paddy wagon drove up. "Waikīkī first," came the shout from the driver. An officer from the receiving desk drove us to our foot beats in the same paddy wagon that transported drunks, transients, and other less-than-favorite sons and daughters of the city. I remember being pensive as we waited for the paddy wagon to return from its Waikīkī run, and I stood slightly alone and away from the others, who glanced at me as if I were the condemned standing at the gallows and it wasn't polite to stare. The wagon came back, and we climbed in and bounced off to downtown. After some minutes, the wagon stopped. The driver came around and opened the door (it didn't open from the inside—prisoners rode in there) and said, "Beat One."

I climbed down, actually feeling afraid. My tension wasn't helped any when my comrades quietly said, "Good luck, bruddah," with the "it was nice knowing ya" tone in their voices. The wagon drove off and I felt very alone.

Well, here I am, I said to myself. Then, *What the hell am I doing here?* Then I remembered what Sergeant Sua, who was assigned to the downtown beats that night, said to us: "Your first night on the beat. You may be a little scared, but never ever show 'em that you're scared." And so I started walking down King Street. And I never forgot his advice the millions of times that I was a little scared.

I remember clearly that when I turned into the housing project, the first person I met was a woman sitting outside her apartment. It was dark, and the porch light barely illuminated her. She gave me a big smile and said, "Hello, officer." Very shortly afterward, a bunch of young kids ran up all smiles and began asking questions about my gun and equipment. And a man in dirty work clothes smiled and nodded. Some older kids stared and walked away. It didn't take long for me to relax a little and feel that public housing or not, people were people. In spite of the friendly people, I couldn't shake a feeling of underlying tension there and the potential for something bad to happen. Looking back, I'm certain that the public's image of the project contributed to its problems.

So I walked. And walked and walked. And in one of my routes through the project I noticed Sergeant Sua parked on the street. Just watching. It felt good to see him there, and I realized that I really wasn't alone. I've preached this again and again to other recruits and students in the college courses I've taught: police work is not a solitary job. It's a job that requires teamwork. It's a job that demands that you trust your beat partner and fellow officers to be there when you need them.

The other memorable thing that happened that night was a homicide—possibly a sign of things to come for me, since years later I would have the privilege of being the lieutenant in charge of the Homicide Detail. A call came over the radio that a stabbing had occurred at the Zamboanga Theater, which showed movies in Filipino. I ran from the housing toward the Zamboanga, which was on King Street less than a quarter mile away, but by the time I got there many other officers and other sergeants I had never seen before were already there and bustling about. A handcuffed Filipino man was sitting on the sidewalk with several officers standing over him. The ambulance crew was packing up to go get the City and County doctor and bring him back to make the pronouncement of death. The body was inside, and I was trying to think of a way to get inside to take a look.

No such luck. Sergeant Sua arrived and seemed pleased to see me there. I was pleased that he seemed pleased. But he assigned me to

The old Zamboanga Theater on King Street, across from the Mayor Wright Housing Project

stand a post about fifteen yards down the sidewalk and keep people from coming any closer to the theater. I stood there for a couple of hours listening to Filipino men talking and wished I could understand what they were saying. Then Sua returned and instructed me to jump in his car. The night was over. Or so I thought.

"Finish your homicide follow-up report before you go home," he said. "Six copies. Write down everything you did at your post."

I didn't do anything, I thought. *I just stood there. But I bet I looked good.*

4
I Am a Boy

Life as a rookie walking the Hotel Street beats wasn't really that bad. People expected to see police officers in that part of town. The red light district of downtown Honolulu was exactly what it was advertised to be. Bars adult porn and novelty shops, street-corner drug dealers, and sidewalk prostitutes adorned Hotel Street. On any given night there was at least one bar fight that needed breaking up, one town drunk who bothered one person too many, and one form of illegal activity or another happening in plain view on the sidewalks.

Geographical areas of the city were broken up into activity-similar chunks called *sectors*. Normally, a sector had from five to seven motorized beats, and places like downtown and Waikīkī had additional foot beats as well. Downtown was the major part of Sector Five. Sector Five had, in addition to the foot beats, four three-wheeled motorcycle beats and one motor vehicle beat. Before the arrival of the three-wheeled Cushman vehicles, HPD used three-wheeled Harley Davidsons, with the trunk compartment behind the operator's seat. They were loud, they were fast, they were macho, they were Harleys, and we envied the slightly more senior officers who got to ride them. They went where most cars couldn't—down alleys, through traffic, and up onto the sidewalk. Many a brawl was broken up by a loud Harley bearing down on the brawlers—on the sidewalk. Really experienced riders would occasionally lift one of the rear wheels and bounce it off the sides of the buildings, forcing bar patrons back inside and bringing forth a flood of complaints.

Because we rookies were so eager to please, the "regulars" endured us. Drunks, prostitutes, and streetwise drug dealers put up with being asked their names, addresses, and histories all night long

19

The Young Street parking lot for the old police headquarters. A three-wheeled Harley-Davidson motorcycle is in the foreground and a specialists' van is in the background.

by every rookie on the street. Each of those contacts was good for one I.C. Card, a.k.a. Identification Check Card, which was filed to document which so-called "undesirable" was on the street on any particular night—just in case a crime occurred and we needed to "round up the usual suspects." On slow nights, we even spent time with a few of the more sociable characters and got to know a little bit about them.

One very regular customer was a guy named Downtown Bobby. On days when he received his welfare check, Bobby was semihuman. He would get some clean clothes and some food and prepare to drink away the rest of his money. Bobby drank to extreme excess. When he got drunk, he wanted to fight everyone. That in itself wasn't so bad. What made us shrink back from Bobby was that when he was drunk he slobbered. He slobbered really bad. And inevitably, we ended up wrestling with Bobby and getting slobber all over us. A rookie was especially unfortunate if he ran into a drunk and disorderly Downtown Bobby on a day he was wearing a newly dry-cleaned uniform. From time to time, we caught Bobby clean and sober, and we took that opportunity to talk to him, explaining that we would have a much better relationship if he weren't so disorderly when he drank. Why did he drink so much? Bobby explained one day that he drank because he had nothing else. He didn't have family who wanted him. He couldn't find work. He had no life beyond Hotel Street. In fact, he got food only when he was in jail.

One night Bobby was drunk, slobbering, and throwing punches at people outside Two Jacks Bar. We were becoming "seasoned rookies," and I remember telling Bobby to knock it off before he got arrested. He seemed to recognize me, and for a moment I thought he was about to behave. He said he "never eat in a couple of days" and needed to go to jail. Then he threw a punch at me. I grabbed him around the neck, but before I could apply the choke hold, another rookie drew his Mace and sprayed Bobby, me, and at least two other bystanders. We finally got Bobby cuffed and into the blue-and-white. The receiving desk captain made us brief him through a narrow crack in his door because the smell of the Mace was affecting anyone who came within three feet of us.

One group of town regulars whom we came to know and to develop a tenuous relationship with were the downtown transvestites, men who dressed up as women, in full-on gowns, jewelry, hose, heels, and a ton of makeup. At times we even commented to each other that a particular transvestite was extraordinarily good-looking. And because it was sometimes difficult to tell if that person was male or female, there was a law on the books that required a man who dressed as a woman to wear a button that read, "I am a boy." I don't believe it was because of any direct discrimination against transvestites; rather, it was because transvestites were occasionally murdered by "dates" who thought a he was a she. Many of the transvestites were prostitutes who looked for easy tricks among drunk, unsuspecting men. Whatever the intent, the "I am a boy" buttons were discrimination against a class of people. Eventually, that law was repealed.

The regular transvestites, who usually hung around The Glades nightclub on Hotel Street, had a relationship with the downtown officers. Part of that relationship was based on mutual need. There were times when the transvestites needed the authority of the police to chase away someone who was harassing them. Most of the downtown transvestites were tough as nails in a fight. But they preferred not to fight, so they called us. And there were times, on the other hand, when an officer needed help in a brawl or with a disorderly drunk. When a couple of "the girls" showed up, their mere presence and reputation in a fight would be enough to deescalate the incident.

One night my partner and I responded to a call reporting a disorderly male at The Glades. We got there quickly, and because there were two of us, no one else was sent immediately. The disorderly male was a very drunk, old, one-legged man on crutches and with a patch over one eye. He was leaning against the lava rock wall entrance to The Glades arguing with the bouncers. Upon our arrival, the bouncers said "Thanks" and retreated just inside the club. We took over.

"Come on, they want you to leave. Let's go."

"F— you."

"No, you don't understand. You have to leave."

He swung a crutch at us. That was our cue, and we pounced into action. We were going to arrest this man for his drunkenness and disorderly conduct. What we failed to consider was that the old guy had been in more bar fights than we realized. He swung the crutch with professional aim. He bounced around the sidewalk on one foot, stuck us with one crutch, and whacked us with the other. My partner got in tight and managed to yank one crutch from his grasp, but the old guy threw himself into me, slamming me against the lava rock wall. The old guy never lost his footing, even on one foot, but my partner and I managed to hit the ground at least once each. We really didn't want to hurt the old man, but it was getting a bit embarrassing, so my partner tried to put a choke hold on him. He wasn't successful because the old guy was twisting and punching and swinging his remaining crutch. I noticed my arm was bleeding where it slammed into the lava rock, and my uniform pants were torn where they caught on the wall's jagged edges. To put it frankly, the old guy was kicking our butts. I was beginning to think we might have to shoot him when a couple of "girls" appeared and started screaming at the old man to knock it off before they got mad.

"They started it," he said, as we pulled his arms behind his back and cuffed him.

"Sit down, Ronald they're going to be nice to you now, aren't you officers?"

I don't remember if his name was Ronald or not, but we *were* nice to Ronald or whoever he was. He was taken to the police station, booked for disorderly conduct, and released on bail. He probably went right back to The Glades, but behaved this time.

My partner and I went to the City and County doctor at the Beretania side of the police station and were treated for sliced arms, cut lips, bruised eyes, and damaged pride.

Sergeant Joy explained to the troops the next day in lineup that we made an arrest at The Glades. My partner and I agreed that he didn't need to point out that the arrested guy was seventy-eight years old, partially blind and crippled, and sent two police officers to the hospital.

That was exaggerating a bit. It wasn't a hospital. It was more like a clinic.

5
Waikīkī on Foot

Walking a foot beat in Waikīkī was completely different from the downtown experience. It required a vastly different approach. The majority of the people were tourists, and the shop owners weren't catering to a sleazy side of life. Oh, there were elements of the downtown drug and prostitute culture, to be sure—just with a different face. The street dealers hung around the back streets or in the "jungle," a tightly clustered neighborhood farther down the Diamond Head side of Waikīkī, composed of old houses and cottages, and the prostitutes looked cleaner and a lot more sober.

The first difference we noticed in Waikīkī, if we were accustomed to walking downtown, was that we could go into a clean restaurant and eat on a clean table and sit on clean seats. We could even eat at a McDonald's if we wanted. (Usually, we didn't eat downtown. It didn't seem like a place where we wanted to put anything into our mouths.) The second difference we noticed was that our uniforms stayed cleaner a lot longer. Being sent to a brawl was rare. Instead, we assisted many a tourist. In fact, we even had a stationary post at the old International Market Place (IMP) for that very purpose.

The IMP was a landmark of beautiful trees and restaurants and shops that blended into the tropical Hawaiian setting. It was a wide-open oasis in the middle of concrete and glass. Okay, it was also a tourist trap. And where there are lots of tourists there are more property crimes and lost people. The IMP post was a nice change from walking. It gave us a chance to meet and speak to people. "How do you get to . . . ?" "Tomorrow we'd like to go to Hanauma Bay. Can we do that by bus?" "Can we walk to the Polynesian Cultural Center from here?" Inevitably, a police officer from another state would come up and want to swap shoulder patches with us, or talk about what it was like to be an officer in Hawai'i. In many mainland departments, the foot beat was prized by the senior officers, and the rookies drove city vehicles. We didn't like to admit we had less than a year on the force.

The pace in Waikīkī was different, too. It was faster. Lots of activity, lots of people, and lots of cars. The opportunity to issue a parking tag was there. In fact, I gave my first parking tag in Waikīkī. I felt funny writing it because I knew I was creating a bill for someone who probably wasn't expecting it. That worry didn't last, though. When I found an illegally parked car, I tagged it. Occasionally, I found a car with expired license plates. Hell, that was considered a moving citation, even if the car was abandoned. I got to use my moving citation book. I even got to use my radio—my big, bulky Motorola that hung like a five-pound weight on my belt. I politely asked the radio dispatcher to check the license plate to see if the car was stolen. I even called her "Ma'am" when I thanked her—no matter how grouchy she sounded. It was rare for a foot patrol officer to find a stolen car, but when one of us did, the others were extremely jealous. *Jeez, why can't I find a stolen car?*

In addition to that "portable" Motorola radio, we carried lots of other things on our belts or in special pockets in our pants. Our guns, obviously. And at least twelve more rounds of ammunition. Lots of guys carried more than twelve. Handcuffs, Mace, a baton or blackjack (they were legal then), and a flashlight. Rounding out our belt items were our whistles, call boxes, and handcuff keys. The call box key was a four-inch skeleton key used to open call boxes and traffic device boxes. Before portable radios became common equipment, beat officers used call boxes to report to the station or get assignments. All these items weighed a few pounds, and not only did we carry them, but we also ran and occasionally wrestled suspects while carrying them. Because we often needed both hands—when writing a tag for example—we learned to hold our flashlights in our armpits. And effectively too, I might add.

Running was always a problem. We carried so much equipment we were afraid we would drop something. The whistles, handcuffs, and call box keys were always coming out of our belts, and we had to be especially aware of them or we would be writing reports to our sergeants explaining why we so carelessly lost those important items. Another problem was that our old holsters were attached on hinges that allowed the holsters to swing, enabling us to sit comfortably but creating a motion problem when we were running. We learned to run while hanging on to items on our belts.

An expired license plate was not the only moving tag we gave. We had to cite pedestrians for jaywalking. This required more courage. We had to stop and detain a living human being and give that person a tag for walking across the street. I remember backing up a beat partner as he gave one such tag. It went something like this.

"Excuse me, sir, please stop."

"Oh, yeah, what's up, officer?"

"Sir, you jaywalked. May I see your driver's license?"

"What?"

"Sir, I'm citing you for jaywalking. May I see your driver's license?"

"What I need one driver's license for cross the street?"

"May I see an ID?"

"I no more one ID. And you really tagging me for crossing the street?"

"Yes, sir, you jaywalked."

"Everybody cross the street here. There, there look, he's crossing over there. Go tag him."

"I'm with you now, sir. Do you have an ID?"

"Chicken shit."

"What was that, sir?"

"No. I no more one ID."

"And what's your name, sir?"

"Ah, John."

"John, what's your last name?"

"Ah, ah, Smith."

"John Smith?"

"Yeah, yeah. John Smith."

"And where do you live, Mr. Smith?"

And so it went on until my partner wrote down all the phony information and handed the jaywalking tag to "John Smith," who promptly thanked us, stuffed the tag in his pocket, and walked away. Smiling. Years later, Mayor Frank Fasi promoted a beautification effort in Honolulu, and the police were asked to cite people for littering. Our leaders demanded several litter tags a day from each officer, to show the mayor that we were an integral part of the project. It was rumored (no one could ever prove it) that many a John Smith from various naval vessels in Pearl Harbor was cited for throwing a paper cup, or cigarette butt, or soda can into the street. How coincidental that all those sailors had the same name and none of them had any form of identification with them.

The life of a Fourth Watch rookie was limited to those areas of police work available to him on foot: giving parking tags and occasional citations for moving violations, responding to a few reports of lost or stolen property, and helping tourists. But one guy from our recruit class took it to a different level. I was walking on Kūhiō Avenue with a beat partner. It was about 0130. It was slow all around. Suddenly we heard a police whistle blowing frantically just down the road. We looked in the direction of the shrill blasts and saw a car coming toward us with an officer running in the road behind it, blowing his whistle and waving his flashlight. My partner and I stepped into the road and waved for the car to stop. He pulled over. A motorcycle beat officer coming in the opposite direction saw us and also stopped. The running officer caught up to us a few seconds later.

"What happened?" the motorcycle cop asked.

"He . . . he was . . . he was speeding," the running rookie managed to get out between breaths.

"He was speeding?" asked the astonished motorcycle cop. "How you know he was speeding?"

"I've been watching the flow of traffic. This guy was going faster than them."

The senior cop looked at the rookie and then at the driver. "Brah, you can go."

He started up his motorcycle, stared pitifully at the breathless rookie standing in the street, and as he drove off, said, "If you try to stop one more car, I'm going to tag you myself."

Ah, the rookie's life in Waikīkī.

6
Rookie Ridealong

The Honolulu Police Department is one of the very few departments in which officers drive their own cars on duty. Most other departments prefer officers to drive government-owned cars. In Honolulu, officers are given a stipend called a *motor allowance* in return for using their own cars. This stipend is supposed to cover all expenses: the cost of the car, maintenance, and a portion of the insurance. I have never met an officer whose motor allowance was enough to cover the expense of the car. The City and County of Honolulu gets off cheap in this respect, but many officers prefer to drive a car of their choice from the approved list. Think of it. Back in 1971, the city cars didn't have a radio or air-conditioning. An officer shared the car with whoever else drove it—and subsequently got their mess—and had to transport prisoners in the backseat. If we drove our own cars, we had air, a stereo system, and the comforts of our own cars without having to transport prisoners. Still, there were some drawbacks.

The first thing we did when we bought a new car and put it into service was have the radio shop technicians remove the headliner and carpeting to install a radio and a blue light. They drilled holes in the dash to mount the radio and siren switch, and in 1971, drilled holes in the roof and trunk fender to mount the blue light and radio antenna. It was very difficult to watch and listen to the drill grind the metal away as it tore into the roof. The radio shop techs strongly suggested that we drop the car off and return in three hours. By then we would have a newly installed radio, blue light, and siren. With new technology and better equipment, less drilling and fewer broken hearts occur than in the early seventies, when officers watched their

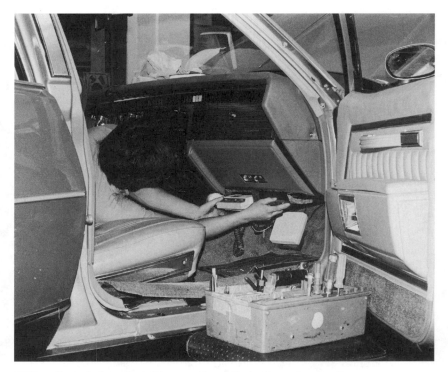

HPD radio technician installing a police radio in the early seventies

brand new Oldsmobile Cutlass Supremes pounded, drilled, and bent as they were transformed into police cars.

A couple of months into the Fourth Watch, we were surprised with the news that we would get to ride with seasoned officers. This would accustom us to motorized patrol and to life on the shifts. I remember two very different Fourth Watch ridealongs.

My first ridealong was with Officer Lee Dempsey. When we were introduced to each other, he was parked on Young Street. He got in on the driver's side and I got in on the passenger's side. You know how, when the curb is a lot higher than normal and you get into a car, the car sinks a little and the car's door is now at the level of the sidewalk, and when you pull the door shut it scrapes against the concrete? Yup, that was our first intimate moment on duty together. It was a brand new car. Oldsmobile 442. Brand new. I guess after a while the memory of the sound of the door scraping on the concrete faded and we talked about police work. I don't remember much about that particular night except for that close encounter with the passenger door. And parking in the zoo parking lot. You know how, when you're a smoker and you light your cigarette with a match from a folding matchbook, and you cup your hands together to block the wind from putting your match out, and the folding matchbook is in your palm, the match you lit accidentally ignites the rest of the matches in the matchbook, and you have this small, yet very hot flash fire in your cupped hands, and your hands get burned and you drop the burning matchbook onto your lap and it starts to burn your pants, and you swish it off onto the floor of the passenger seat of a brand new Oldsmobile 442? Yup. Brand new. Thank God for the plastic floor mats covering his carpet.

One of the bennies of riding with senior officers is that they know where to eat. They're like truck drivers. Police officers and truck drivers know all the holes-in-the-wall and greasy spoons and other good places to eat. But when you're a police officer you learn to eat very quickly. Inevitably, an important call will come in just as you start to eat. Many a lunch gets tossed into the can because of business. Which was the case one evening in Hawai'i Kai.

I don't remember the name of the officer I was riding with, but we had just settled into a couple of plate lunches. It was dark, sometime near 2100, and we were both hungry.

"Central calling nine-one."

"Nine-one standing by."

"A possible burg in progress at one twenty-three Hawai'i Kai Drive." (I don't remember the actual address.)

"Proceeding." (The lunches went into the can.)

"Central calling nine-two and nine-four."

"Nine-two proceeding."

"Nine-four proceeding."

We all got to the area of the house very quickly. My mentor that night gave me quick instructions: go left around the side of that house and check the back side of a series of houses. He was going right. The other two officers were doing the same thing a couple of houses down from us. I was picking up quickly on his experience.

"Nine-one, Central."

"Standing by."

"Call back the owners. Do they still see the suspect? Any description?"

And he was gone, running toward the right side of the house. I quickly understood. We would get more info from Dispatch telling us if we were in the right vicinity.

I ran down the left side of the house and swung my flashlight beam along the building. My heart almost stopped. There he was, crouched in the shadows of the house. As soon as my light hit him he was running.

"I got him at the back of the house," I shouted into the portable radio as I pursued him.

The would-be burglar sprinted toward the canal and began running on a fairly wide rock wall that abutted the canal. I could see my partner running toward us down the right side of the house. The burglar was almost within my reach as he swung himself around the six-foot wooden fence that jutted about a foot out past the rock wall over the canal. The fence separated the yards of two houses. I didn't even slow down. I grabbed the top of the wall and swung myself through the air around the wall. *You are NOT getting away from me,* I thought.

You know how, when you grab a wooden fence jutting about a foot over a canal and expect to swing around it to the continuation of the rock wall on the other side, but the rock wall is not there because the continuation of the property line is set back about ten feet for the property next door, and you're too heavy to hold yourself up against the fence, and the force of your swinging pulls you away from the fence and you fall on top of the suspect in the water?

I caught him. Got soaking wet, but I caught him. My mentor was shining his flashlight into the water, and two other officers were in the backyard of the house with the short property line. Someone was shouting for the suspect to give it up and climb out. I had him by the shirt and was pushing him into the rock wall. He kept saying, "Okay, okay, okay." I guess he worried that he was about to be stomped or something. He climbed out and was handcuffed. I climbed out, and one of the officers said something like, "Yeah, go get him." A woman came out of the house and offered me a towel. The suspect was instructed to sit on the driveway as we awaited the blue-and-white that was coming to drive him in. My mentor took the information needed for the report from the homeowners. He was eyeing me suspiciously, and I wondered if he thought I was shirking my duties. I told him my notebook was soaked and useless but that I would take the info if he had a spare notebook. "No, no," he said, "don't worry about it."

A few minutes later the blue-and-white came up. The driver searched the suspect again and put him into the back of the car. He was about to drive off when my mentor shouted, "Wait! Wait!"

I found out then why he was eyeing me up.

"Dias. You not going be offended if you go in with the blue-and-white, eh? I got cloth seats."

That was it. I was still pretty wet, and he was worried about his seats and my wet pants. Well, it wasn't a problem for me. I would have felt the same.

Soaking wet, I still felt good. This was a first for me. Catching a crook during an "in-progress" case.

7
Receiving Desk

Our days on the Fourth Watch were numbered. We had been there some months now and were expecting another recruit class to graduate and replace us. That meant assignment to the other watches, or to another district, like Pearl City or Kāne‘ohe or Wahiawā, or to a nonpatrol assignment such as Records Division or Communications Division (Dispatch). We shuddered at the thought of being assigned to a nonpatrol division. We would be clerks, we thought, not police officers.

One day, Sergeant Sua announced in lineup that he had our new assignments, and that effective the following Sunday, we would all be assigned to new posts. We did well, he said. He was pleased with our performance, he said. He would miss us, he said. It was a happy, yet melancholy time. The familiar was being replaced with something new again. A few months earlier we had moved from recruit school to the Fourth Watch, and now our home was changing again. But we knew that this was the real beginning. Prior to these new assignments, we were still connected to our socialization process; we were becoming police officers. It was like growing up and becoming adults. It didn't happen overnight, yet one day we knew we were there. That was how we felt that day.

Sergeant Sua read the assignments, making sure each rookie understood where he was to report on Sunday. Sergeant Joy stood off to the side, smiling contentedly and nodding his approval at each assignment.

"Dias."

"Sir!"

"Bravo Watch."

"Yes, sir!" *Oh, thank you!* I was not going to a nonpatrol assignment.

But Sergeant Sua moved his glasses lower on his nose and looked at me.

"Receiving desk."

"Sir." I said aloud. *Shit,* I thought privately, for a second time during the Fourth Watch.

The receiving desk, while assigned to District One Patrol, was an inside job. I was not pleased. The function of the desk was to process arrested persons—people arrested by other police officers who had other, more exciting jobs. Well, it wouldn't be forever.

I reported for duty and was shown the various processes by an officer who smiled constantly. I learned later that he was smiling because that was his last night on the desk. I was his replacement. He was being motorized and moved to a field assignment. I asked him how long he had been assigned to the desk. "Two years," he said. *Two years! My God, how could he stand it? Two years! How long would it be for me?*

The receiving desk handles duties more complex than simply booking a prisoner. When a prisoner was brought into the desk, he or she was searched and placed into a holding cell. The arresting officer then conferred with the watch captain, who also oversaw the receiving desk. If the arrest was approved, the booking process began. The prisoner was brought out to a desk. We typed (not many computers then) a booking report that contained the biographical data on the prisoner and some basic facts regarding the offense for which he or she was arrested. The one computer we did have was hooked up to our arrest file. We checked the electronic file to see if the prisoner had prior arrests. If not, he was assigned a booking number, called an Alpha number. It read something like this: A-43278. It was a number assigned only to a single prisoner and would follow him all his life. If he was arrested years later, his Alpha number would be located and logged on the booking report.

After the booking report was completed, we took the prisoner to

The receiving desk at the old police headquarters. The male holding cells are to the right and the female cell is the second door.

another room and took inked fingerprints from him. These were submitted to the Records Division, where they were compared with any on file. One copy was sent to FBI headquarters in Washington, D.C., for their records. After the fingerprinting, the prisoner was moved to a different part of the room and his mug photo was taken. His Alpha number and the date were included in the photo in plastic letters and numbers on a little board held in front of him. Finally, the prisoner was brought back into the booking area to await bail, or if no bail was forthcoming, taken to the cell block.

The cell block was like a tunnel. It had no windows. The doors were heavy steel, and the bars were one inch in diameter. The walls were painted brown, and the lighting was poor. It was cold and damp and cavelike. Everything echoed. There was one room with multiple beds for the trusties—inmates from Oʻahu Prison who were given good-behavior status and allowed to work in the cell block, cleaning and assisting the cook. There were rows of individual cells, one very large room for multiple prisoners, a section for female prisoners, and two padded cells for disorderly people.

And disorderly people we had. My first, uninformed impression of assignment to the desk was that it would be like a clerk's job. I didn't realize how wrong I was. I got into more fights, got punched more frequently, and dirtied and damaged my uniform more than I did the entire time I was a motorized patrol officer. The receiving desk was a busy, disorderly, and abusive place to work.

On one night shift, a very large Polynesian man who had been arrested for assaulting a police officer was brought in. He was over six feet four inches tall and easily weighed more than 250 pounds; his arms were as big as my thighs. He was very unhappy and uncooperative. He had a gash on his forehead at his hairline, but he refused treatment. The blood on his head and face was drying, but the wound was oozing a little, slowly adding a fresh layer of blood to his face.

We were proceeding with the booking process slowly when the man's BIG brother showed up at the bail-out window. He not only appeared to be older, but he also was taller and heavier than his younger brother. And stronger, we were soon to learn. The two began to shout at each other in their South Pacific language, and the bigger brother accused us of hurting his brother. The big guy inside was actually crying, and this further enraged the bigger guy outside. He was shouting, "Let me in!" but we wouldn't open the door, which made him even angrier.

Our captain that night was an older, slender man who had served many years in nonpatrol assignments and was nearing the end of his career. Captain K.'s office was adjacent to the desk and opened into the waiting area where the smaller brother stood. The bigger man could see that the captain's office was a way to get through into the desk area, so he slammed his shoulder into the captain's door and burst it open. Before we could react, the man grabbed Captain K., pulling him over the desk and punching him in the head several times, knocking him out. We rushed into the captain's office and tried to subdue the man. One officer took out his blackjack and was swinging it all around. He broke a few bones in my right hand doing that, and it only seemed to make the man even angrier. While this was happening, the man's younger, but still-large brother began to flip desks in the booking area and fought with the other half of the officers assigned to the receiving desk. In seconds, we were in a fight we had not expected, and for a few minutes, it seemed we were losing. Someone, however, had the good sense to call dispatch and report a "ten-fifteen at the receiving desk."

Ten-fifteen was code for "Officer in trouble, send help immediately." Soon, field officers from Sectors Six, Seven, and Eight were converging on the desk. With their help we regained control and got both brothers into the cell block. When the dust cleared, we had multiple officers with injuries, and several officers, including Captain K. and me, were taken to the hospital. The incident affirmed the notion that HPD is the "biggest gang in town." We took our lumps but called in help and resolved the problem. In other words, we won this fight. But physical force need not be the only resolution to violence. Sometimes, negotiation is much more successful, as I would learn later in my career.

On another night at the desk, a disorderly woman was brought in. She was one of our regulars. A young woman with an alcohol problem, Vicky was nearly uncontrollable when officers brought her to the desk and locked her into the women's holding cell. She was Caucasian, in her early twenties, with shoulder-length blond hair, and I imagined she would be attractive when she wasn't drunk. But tonight she smelled of alcohol and looked as if she had not bathed in a week. A female Downtown Bobby.

Booking processes were the same for men and women. The major difference was the search. Each prisoner had to be searched for weapons. This was critical. We couldn't have a prisoner pull out a knife and attack one of us. Since we were working so closely with prisoners, the risk of injury was great, so everyone was searched. Normally, police matrons helped with the women prisoners. The department had no female patrol officers at that time, and the matrons had the desk duty of booking and searching women prisoners. When a matron was not available, the searching fell to male officers. No matron was available that night, so booking Vicky fell to me.

Searching a prisoner involved touching and feeling the person's body, hair, and clothing for any object that could be a weapon. The prisoner was asked to stand facing the wall, spread his feet apart, and lean forward so his hands were on the wall. We started with the head, feeling the hair, running our fingers around the collar, feeling front, back, sides of the shirt. We checked the waistband, ensuring that nothing was hidden behind or in the belt or buckle. (Some buckles actually are designed as knives.) Then we checked the groin, pants, and shoes. After the search, we were supposed to feel comfortable that the prisoner had no weapon hidden on him. Searching a woman was no different, except we used the back of the hand, never the fingers or palm, to feel the body and clothing. We usually had another officer witness the process to ensure we didn't do anything that was disrespectful and to counter any false claims that we did.

Vicky was in the women's holding cell, and I opened the door and asked her to come out so we could complete the booking process. She walked toward me, and as soon as she was in range she punched me in the face. I was standing at the threshold of the cell when she punched me. I absorbed the blow, grabbed her shoulder, and spun her away from me. Instinctively, I applied the choke hold. I expected Vicky to pass out quickly, since she was so drunk. Instead, however, Vicky reached behind her with her right hand and grabbed me between the legs. She managed to get a tight grip on my groin. No sense mincing words, she had me by my testicles and was squeezing and twisting really hard.

Women reading this may not fully appreciate the pain that occurs when one has one's testicles squeezed and twisted, but I think the men will. They'll understand the stabbing pain shooting into my abdomen, the weakness in my legs, the beads of sweat bursting onto my forehead, my redness of face, the feeling of panic as the grip does not lessen.

"Let . . . go," I managed to grunt.

"You let go," she responded.

I am not losing this battle, I thought, and I squeezed my arm on her neck and pushed her head forward as hard as I could.

Vicky squeezed and twisted my testicles as hard as she could in response.

I eased up a little and she followed suit.

"Will you behave?" I groaned through clenched teeth.

Vicky nodded yes.

"Okay. We both let go, okay?"

Vicky nodded yes.

"On three. One, two, three."

I let go. Vicky let go. I leaned heavily on one side of the door frame and she on the other, catching our breaths. The pain still shot into my stomach, and my legs were still weak.

"Go sit down by the typewriter."

She did, and I joined her a few seconds later. I began the booking process. I still needed to win the battle.

"Next time, don't hit a police officer," I scolded, making sure I had, at least, the last word.

8
Motorized At Last

Much to my everlasting gratitude, I spent only seven months working on the receiving desk. With the departmental increases in staffing, the patrol divisions needed officers, and in the fall of 1972 I was assigned as a motor-patrol officer to District Four, Kāneʻohe. While the headquarters was in Kāneʻohe, the district covered the entire windward coast from the Makapuʻu Lighthouse to the end of the Kahuku district. It was just another assignment, but I saw it as a promotion. Which of course it wasn't. While I was very happy to leave the receiving desk, I had a problem. The car I owned at that time was a Datsun. A small, yellow Datsun. I needed, within two weeks, an American car that was on the approved list. To add to my problem, Honolulu was in the middle of a shipping strike. Add to that the fact that I wasn't making much money. I never gave any thought to a used car. It had to be new, of course. A newly motorized patrol officer needed a new car

So I went to Aloha Motors. There are probably people reading this who bought many a car from Aloha Motors. And a few who never heard of the place. Aloha Motors was a landmark institution that stood on the same spot the convention center stands on today. Over the years I bought three cars from Aloha Motors. But this first one was the most important because it was going to be the first. As it turned out, I had no choice. Aloha Motors had only one car on its lot that met department requirements: a 1972 Chevelle, and I paid less than six thousand dollars for it. I'll tell you more about this car a little later. Suffice it to say I wasn't happy. But I had wheels.

I endured the transition from civilian car to police car fairly well. I guess I wasn't so bothered with all the drilling and tearing and bending because I wasn't all that excited about the car. I was more excited that I was being motorized.

One other officer from my recruit class was assigned to District Four. Heleman Kaonohi and I were both assigned to the third shift, as swing officers. In other words, we were not given a permanent beat. That was reserved for more senior officers. We filled in wherever we were needed—Waimānalo, Kailua, Kāne'ohe, or the North Shore. That first night though, we were assigned to Kāne'ohe town. Nothing special happened that first night, except that both Heleman and I were sent to a domestic argument on a street I never heard of. We both responded to the dispatcher that we were proceeding, and both of us immediately began a search of our map books. The dispatcher said it was off Kahekili Highway, but I couldn't find it. For about five minutes, Heleman and I whizzed past each other on Kahekili, turned around, and whizzed past each other again. It was taking way too long for us to find this residence, and apparently other officers assigned to Kāne'ohe thought so too. They responded, and after resolving the problem there, returned to their beats. Heleman and I pulled off the roadway onto a wide shoulder, our cars facing opposite directions so we could talk to each other, both of us embarrassed that we never found the house—and both determined that it would not happen again. And the way to make it not happen again was to drive the streets on our beat. Patrol, patrol, patrol, and learn the names of every street we're on, especially the small, narrow, out-of-the-way streets.

Cops driving on roadways have the same effect on law-abiding people as they do on crooks. Say you're on the freeway doing sixty-five. You suddenly see a cop in your rearview mirror. You slow down. The cop takes an off ramp. What do you do? Usually, you speed back up to sixty-five or more. Same with a crook. The crook is casing a house. He's just about ready to break in. A cop appears. The crook cools it until the cop leaves the area; then he burglarizes the house. Same concept.

The problem with freeway drivers nowadays is that they don't slow down. None of them. Everyone on the H-1 in the Pearl City area does eighty to eighty-five. A cop shows up, no effect. They figured it out. If everyone speeds thirty miles per hour over the speed limit, who's the cop going to stop and tag?

But every now and again a cop on a highway *will* have an effect on traffic. I was driving home on the H-3 the other day in a group of five or six cars. We were all doing sixty-five to seventy. Then a solo motorcycle cop came flying up on us with his blue running lights on. Everyone slowed to fifty-five. The cop was behind two rows of cars, weaving from lane to lane. I wondered at first if he was heading off to a case or an accident and wanted to get past us, but if that were so, he could have turned on his flashing blue lights and we all would have got out of his way. After a mile or so, it became evident that we were simply going too slow for him. And no one dared take the chance that he wouldn't tag the first one of us to speed up. He changed lanes behind us for about six miles until he found an opening at the Kamehameha Highway off ramp in Kāne'ohe and took off like a bat out of hell. Sure, he was a poor example for other motorists, but we've all driven over that speed limit a few times, haven't we?

Chief Michael Nakamura tried to change that image by having officers on the force slow down during his term. He drove the speed limit on the freeways on his way home, and whenever an off-duty officer passed him, he got the license plate number and notified that officer's commander to remind the officer to obey the speed limit. It worked. When the CEO is on the road paying attention to how his employees are driving the filter-down effect is tremendous.

At the start of my District Four assignment, I was teamed with a gentleman and beat partner named Ronnie, who swore he knew me from somewhere. I didn't remember knowing Ronnie before that assignment, so I was certain he was mistaken. At least once a week, though, he would come up with a different location, a different potential mutual friend, something that would jar his or my memory, but with no luck. Then one day, he walked into lineup with a wide grin on his face and announced that he remembered where he knew me from.

"I tagged you on Likelike Highway," he jubilantly proclaimed. "I was in solo bikes and you were speeding."

He was right. It all came back then. Ronnie was a solo motorcycle officer and I was speeding on Likelike Highway. And he tagged me. I was a junior at Damien Memorial High School and I had to appear in juvenile court with my mom. It was a lousy experience. Ronnie smiled and slapped my back.

"I knew I knew you from someplace."

I was hoping against hope that Ronnie would not remember that he was the same solo bike officer who tried to tag me again on University Avenue. I was attending the University of Hawai'i and driving to classes. I had just come off the freeway and was headed mauka on University. The entire group of cars I was in was speeding, and no one saw the cop come up on us. He passed me and pulled alongside the car in front of me. I watched him point to the driver and then to the side of the road, signaling the driver to pull over.

"Hah," I thought. "He got him."

Then he turned on his seat as he drove forward and pointed to me and then to the side of the road. It was then that I recognized him as the same guy who tagged me on Likelike Highway. I panicked. Another speeding tag would send my insurance into deep space. And I probably would get a crack or two from my parents.

The guy ahead of me pulled over on University just past Dole Street. The cop pulled over behind him. I turned right. My earlier panic was nothing compared with the terror I felt after I turned onto Dole. *If the cop comes after me, he'll arrest me,* I thought.

I turned into the first narrow lane I saw and disappeared among some old UH buildings. I stopped and waited for the sound of a motorcycle. It never came. I finally built up the courage to start my car and drive out, half expecting to find a hundred cops searching for me all over the UH area. I didn't get to school that day; I was too nervous. If I had realized that all he needed to do was get my license number, I would never have run. I did what I did because I was young and I panicked. My advice is, never, never run from a police officer. Consequences always become more severe when that happens.

"Yeah, Ronnie, I remember now," I said. I was sweating profusely. "I was speeding and I deserved that tag."

Ronnie nodded. "Yeah, but you showed respect and stopped. I hate it when guys run away from a tag. I never forget them, either."

I smiled and nodded. Perspiration was dripping off my nose and chin. Ronnie still had his big smile. He slapped my back again and walked into the squad room for lineup.

9
Whose Fire Is It Anyway?

There is a myth floating around that when a person becomes a police officer he suddenly knows everything there is to know. He gets asked all kinds of questions on all types of topics and is expected to have the correct answers. The fact is, the vast majority of officers are normal, everyday folk with their own individual levels of intelligence, or lack thereof. We become educated through our schooling, like everyone else, and we become socialized through our experiences, like everyone else. Some people have more experiences and are more worldly than others, and this holds true for police officers as well.

The early seventies, you may remember, brought a gasoline shortage. This created long lines at the pumps and inventive efforts to avoid that extra, unnecessary mile. It also created thieves with gasoline breath.

On one quiet night in Kāneʻohe, a petty thief decided to steal some gas for his car. With his flexible garden hose in one hand and his five-gallon gas can in the other, he siphoned gasoline from cars in the parking lots of apartment complexes along Kahuhipa Street. He made little effort to hide his activity, and when we confronted him, he tried to convince us he was merely putting gasoline *into* his car. Well, he didn't fool anyone. The old gas can, the garden hose, and the fumes that escaped his lips when he spoke gave him away, and we arrested him for theft. And that's when the problems began.

When we investigate a crime, we're supposed to gather the evidence in the case for later presentation to the court. With all the thefts of gas occurring around town, the department became concerned that its evidence storage rooms would fill with cans of gasoline. Soon, the order was given: no gasoline could be stored as evidence at the police station. Only the can in which the gasoline was stored by the thief could be recovered into evidence. Perhaps you can see the problem that many police officers were faced with. What did they do with the gas? Ideally, they returned it to the owner and put it back into the car from which it came. But what if the suspect siphoned gas from multiple cars, as happened that night? There was no way to know just how much gas was taken from which car.

So somewhere around two in the morning, we took the thief and the can of gas to the Kāneʻohe Police Station.

"You can't submit the gas into evidence," we were told by the desk sergeant.

"We can't give it back. What are we going to do?"

"I don't know, but you can't bring it in here."

"What if we put it into the blue-and-white?"

"No, and you can't put it into your own cars either."

"So, Sarge, what are we going to do?"

"I don't know—just get it out of here." He clearly didn't want the issue to be an issue any longer.

So here we were, two young, inexperienced officers standing in front of the Kāneʻohe Police Station with no clue as to what to do with five gallons of gasoline. Frustrated with the lack of guidance from our desk sergeant, we decided to simply throw the gas away. *Where* we were going to throw it away was now the issue.

Putting it into the storm drain didn't seem right. Spilling it onto the street wasn't right either.

"How about the planter in front of the station?"

"Yeah, I guess so. It'll just get absorbed into the dirt and rock."

"Yeah, okay."

So we poured the gas into the planter. We immediately regretted that decision. Gasoline in a planter up against the station's front wall suddenly didn't seem right. The old cigarette butts in the planter didn't add to our confidence either.

"What if somebody tosses in a cigarette? Might have a fire."

"Yeah. What we gonna do?"

The Kāneʻohe Police Station, circa 1972

"What if we water it down? Should cause the gas to disperse, right?"

"Yeah, that's right. Let's go get a hose."

So we soaked the planter with water. But something still didn't sit right.

"You're sure this is safe?"

"I don't know. One way to find out."

In retrospect, lighting the match and tossing it into the water-filled planter wasn't the best decision of the night. The resulting *whoomph* and instant four-foot blaze streaking up the window sent the desk sergeant flying backward from his chair, spouting a stream of obscenities heard in the basement weight room below.

Shooting the flames with the water hose didn't help much, so someone, much to our dismay, called the fire department. The Kāneʻohe Fire Station, you see, is located catty corner from the Kāneʻohe Police Station, about a football field away. It was 2:30 in the morning, and we figured the firemen weren't going to be thrilled at being wakened to put out a fire started by two obviously fire-illiterate police officers. We were right. They weren't thrilled. But we knew we'd pulled a good one, so we stood back quietly and listened, without comment, to the wisecracks about the need for in-service training on fire prevention.

When the fire was out, the firemen gathered up their extinguishers, climbed back onto the big fire truck, and slowly rolled the hundred yards back to their station house.

We looked at the front wall of the station. It was stained with black soot, and the remnants of white foam floated everywhere—in the planter, on the sidewalk, on the sergeant's window. It was then that the feeling of foolishness *really* began to set in. The silence from the desk sergeant didn t help either. He looked at us now and again and just shook his head.

We typed up our reports as quickly as possible and got out. Morning was coming, and people would be arriving at work. The next shift would be choking on their coffee as they were told the story. Yeah, it was time to leave. We turned in the reports and managed a "Sorry, Sarge," as we walked out the door. The absurdity of the night wasn't over yet, because one of us asked the desk sergeant, "Do you think the major will be upset?" He could only shake his head.

We survived that night, but looking back, I still don't think the firemen had to turn on their siren just to cross the street.

10
In the Dark

As a child I never really liked being alone in the dark. Most kids don't. And most of us take this dislike with us into adulthood. It's something about the dark. Normal sounds seem strange. It's dark.

Half of a patrol officer's working life is in the dark, and we learn to adapt. Our weak hand is our flashlight hand because we want to leave our strong hand free in case we need our weapon. We become accustomed to carrying a flashlight in our armpit when issuing a citation. We adjust our car's interior lights so they stay off when we open the door; we don't want the lights making us a target. We learn to drive with our headlights off, and more than likely, we have a toggle switch that controls our brake lights so we can eliminate them as well.

One effect of working in the dark is that people tend to come together during free time. I've made my checks, the neighborhood streets are quiet, the businesses are closed and locked, traffic is slow, and the road is becoming monotonous. So I call my beat partner on the radio.

"Four-two-six to four-two-seven."

"Four-two-seven by."

"Ten-five for a ten-three?"

Translation: Beat officer 426 calling Beat officer 427. Beat officer 427 standing by for your call. What is your location for a meeting between you and me?

Codes were a big part of life as a beat officer. The Ten Code series—a verbal shorthand—reduced the need for normal speech among officers and dispatchers. Some years ago, however, police agencies recommended that officers simply say what they need to say. In other words, speak plainly and clearly and eliminate confusion.

So I give my location, and my beat partner soon drives up, along with two or three other officers who heard my call and also have nothing to do. Since three or four officers parked in a highly visible location may bring complaints of congregating, the location of the meeting often shifts to out-of-the-way spots the public will not normally drive to at three in the morning. And I really don't need the watch commander driving up and ruining a nice cozy gathering, so I use more codes.

"Ten-three at the big tree."

Translation: Meet me at Hawaiian Memorial Park, second driveway toward Kailua, all the way in the back on the right near the large jacaranda tree. And don't forget to turn off your lights and come in dark. (It's a rookie's error to drive in with headlights on and illuminate everyone else.)

So there we gather, in the dark, and sip coffee and talk story. The conversation covers any and all topics, depending on what's happening that night, who recently got suspended (and we know he didn't deserve it), who got promoted (and we know he didn't deserve it), and on and on. A topic that comes up from time to time is ghost stories. It can come up because someone spoke to an elderly man the other night who went on about how he once saw an old Hawaiian woman dressed all in white with long, flowing white hair standing at the side of the road as he drove past her in Kahaluʻu. But there she was again at Kahana Bay, and again in Hauʻula and again in Kahuku. How could she be at all those places ahead of him as he drove on? And his friend, Wilfred, also saw her a few years ago, and he stopped and picked her up and after driving a few minutes he saw her on the side of the road again and he looked at the passenger seat and she was gone. And she was supposed to be a woman who died mysteriously and now spent her nights walking alongside the road. And he was so sincere in his telling of the tale.

We were parked at Hawaiian Memorial Park one night, swapping ghost stories. Charlie told us about the Old Hauʻula Police Substation. One afternoon a long time ago, when Charlie was a young officer, a young man was arrested and taken to the Hauʻula Substation. Charlie couldn't remember what he was arrested for. The man was booked and put into the holding cell at the rear of the small building. After some time, an officer went back to check on him and found him hanging by a noose fashioned from his blanket. Years later, Charlie said, he and the sector sergeant were in the substation working the night shift. (Isn't it always the night shift?) He was working on a report, and the sergeant was resting with his head on his arms on the table. Suddenly the sergeant jerked up, looked down the hall toward the holding cell, got up, walked to his car, got in, and sped off in the Kāneʻohe direction. Charlie called after him on the radio with no response, then got in his own car and followed. He finally caught up with the sergeant, who was stopped on the side of the road at Chinaman's Hat. He said the sergeant was wide-eyed, and when asked what was wrong said, "Did you see him?"

"I didn't see anyone. What did you see?"

"I heard a noise and looked down the hall and there was a young man walking toward me. He had a cloth tied around his neck. I could see through him."

Everyone had the mandatory goose bumps, and that was the end of Charlie's tale. No one doubted his sincerity, but we all had our own levels of disbelief and our own thoughts about what could have happened. But standing in the dark, in the middle of a cemetery, and hearing about another officer's close call with a ghost does get you to look around a little bit.

Some time later I was assigned one night to the old 434 beat. This beat encompassed the Kahuku area through the UH Research Lab on the North Shore. It was two-thirty or three in the morning. I had a couple of cases, which was rare for that beat and time of night, and I was looking for a quiet place to sit and write my reports. In the early seventies, we hand-wrote our reports in our cars during our spare time. I was driving past the old Turtle Bay Hilton, headed in the

Waimea direction, when I noticed the long driveway and white buildings of Crawford Convalescent Center, commonly called Crawford's Home, a home for the elderly. I pulled in, went down the long driveway, and circled a large tree, whose branches nearly covered the entire turnaround area, making for a quiet, secluded spot to write my reports.

I stopped, but left my engine running and turned on my interior light. I have to tell you here that the car I was driving was that 1972 Chevrolet Chevelle I bought at Aloha Motors. It came right out of a designer's nightmare or maybe warped sense of humor. It was a six-cylinder coupe, automatic, with faux leather seats, crank windows, AM/FM stereo (no cassette), and no air-conditioning. The car was painted a light tan mixed with a light brown and a splash of green and yellow. The top of the dash was green, the face of the dash was brown, the steering wheel was black, the door panels were tan, and the seats were white. We joked that it was put together by a blind guy on a Friday, in the late afternoon.

So there I was, sitting in the driveway of Crawford's Home, facing the street with my driver's side window down and my passenger's side window up and the interior light on. I got my forms together and had just begun to write my report when I heard a noise. I looked to my right out the window, but could see only the reflection of the seat on the window glass. Instinctively, I turned the interior light off to eliminate the reflection, but I could see nothing in the quiet dark of the grounds around the white buildings.

As I turned back in my seat, the corner of my eye caught something just out my door and I looked quickly to my left. There, standing immediately outside my door, was what appeared to be a very old man with long, flowing white hair and a long, flowing white beard. He must have been dressed in white as well because everything about him seemed white, including his face.

I don't remember putting the gearshift lever in drive. I don't remember making the turn out of Crawford's Home onto Kamehameha Highway and heading back toward Kahuku. I don't remember how my notebook and report forms got to the backseat of the car. I do remember that when I passed the Turtle Bay Hilton, I was driving very, very fast. My speedometer said I was doing over a hundred, and the idiot light on my dash told me my parking brake was still on. The smell of burning brake pads filled the car. I slowed down, but kept looking in my rearview mirror into my backseat and the roadway behind. Just to see . . . . I soon pulled into the Chevron station in Lā'ie. My beat partner was parked in the light of the over-hang, and I pulled alongside him. It was some time before I could build the courage to admit what had just transpired.

"Was probably some old man looking for help. You left an old man who needed help standing in the parking lot in the dark. You better go back and see if he needs help."

"Yeah, you're right. Come with me."

"No, I cannot. I'm . . . I'm busy."

"You're not doing anything. It's quiet. Let's go."

"No, it's your beat. You go."

"I know why you don't wanna go."

"Not. I'm busy."

"Nah. Nah. You scared, too!"

"Not."

We never did go. And the old man had plenty of time to ask for help. If he was an old man.

11
Codes and Cop Speak

Back in the seventies, many police departments used (and some still use today) a code system to converse over their radios. Some of these codes are universal. They're known as the Ten Code series, and each code designates one typical police function or phrase. Individual departments may modify some or all the codes to meet their individual needs, based on their culture or requirements or region in the United States. The Honolulu Police Department has a set of codes slightly different from the codes of those of the Association of Public Safety Communication Officials. The most common of HPD's codes are

10-1   "Return to the station."
10-2   "Call me or call this telephone number."
10-3   "Meet with me."
10-4   "Your transmission is acknowledged."
10-5   "What is your location?" or simply "a location."
10-6   "Repeat your last statement."
10-7   "I have arrived at my destination."
10-8   "I have completed my assignment," or "I am leaving my last location."
10-9   "I am off my car at the station house."
10-10 "I need an ambulance at this location."
10-11 "I am on duty."
10-12 "I am on a bathroom break."
10-13 "Call home."
10-14 "Lunch break."
10-15 "Police officer in trouble, needs immediate help."
10-16 "Cancel the last request or transmission."

In addition to using the Ten Code Series, officers and dispatchers commonly use the phonetic alphabet to make communication between field officer and dispatcher perfectly clear. Using the phonetic alphabet eliminates the confusion between the sounds of letters such as F and S or P and T. The standard phonetic alphabet is

A = Alpha	J = Juliet	S = Sierra
B = Bravo	K = Kilo	T = Tango
C = Charlie	L = Lima	U = Uniform
D = Delta	M = Mike	V = Victor
E = Echo	N = November	W = Whiskey
F = Fox trot	O = Oscar	X = X-Ray
G = Golf	P = Papa	Y = Yankee
H = Hotel	Q = Quebec	Z = Zulu
I = India	R = Romeo	

As with the Ten Code Series, individual departments or locales may amend the phonetic alphabet by using words that are common to their culture. In the case of HPD, you find some officers commonly using local words such as Hilo for H, Kona for K, and Maui for M.

And you may think that's it in terms of police codes. Not yet. Another old series of codes identifies specific crimes or situations. Code one refers to a traffic collision. Code ten refers to a stolen vehicle. Code thirty-one is a drunk driver, while code twenty-five is a drunk individual.

So then, that's it? No, there's more. Officers often use shortened words or phrases with their official communications. "Rap" refers to an arrest record, not a musical style, for example.

But it does not end there either. Abbreviations also have a place in cop speak. R.O. stands for the registered owner of a vehicle. M.O. has two meanings. First, it describes the *modus operandi,* Latin for method of operation, or the regular habits of a crook in the course of committing a crime. It can also refer to a person in need of mental observation at a psychiatric unit. Everyone knows U.C. stands for undercover; C.I., for a confidential informant; P.C., for probable cause; and A.P.B., for all points bulletin.

So that must be it. Well, we're getting close. A few other words and phrases used primarily by law enforcement are

Algor mortis:	The cooling of the body after death.
Backup:	A reinforcing or assisting officer.
Bag the hands:	Encase the hands of a homicide victim or shooting suspect to preserve GSR (gunshot residue).
Canvass:	To search a location for witnesses.
Chain of custody:	The documentation of the custody of evidence as it moves between officers through the law enforcement and judicial systems.
Dinosaur:	A police officer unwilling to change old-fashioned ways.
Domestic:	Short for a domestic incident or argument.
Eyeball:	To estimate speed without a laser gun.
Felony:	A crime punishable by more than one year in prison.
Fence:	Someone who buys stolen property and resells it.
Gat:	A handgun.
Hearsay:	Third-person evidence, or what one person heard another say.
Hit-and-run:	Fleeing the scene of a motor vehicle collision.
John:	The client of a prostitute.
Latents:	Hidden fingerprints.
Lividity:	*Livor mortis,* or the settling of the blood after death.
Mirandize:	To advise a suspect of his or her rights against self-incrimination and to have an attorney present when speaking to the police.
Perp:	Short for *perpetrator*.
Probable cause:	Sufficient reason to believe that a crime has been committed.

SWAT:	Special Weapons and Tactics Team.
Tail:	To follow as in a surveillance.
Working girl:	A prostitute.

Police lingo gets its point across quickly and clearly. Most of the time. Here's what an officer might say during a routine vehicle stop:

"Four-two-seven R.O. Code ten on Charlie, Alpha, X-Ray, six-three-nine."

Translation: Beat officer 427 to dispatch. Please conduct a computer check for a stolen vehicle and registered owner on license number CAX 639. Thank you.

The "please" and "thank you" are options that help develop good relations with dispatchers—a practice lost on a few officers, who take themselves too seriously. I'm glad to say that most of our officers in Honolulu are among the most courteous I've met.

All our codes, abbreviations, and phonetic spellings do make for awkward moments though. One day, my beat partner pulled over a young Asian man for a traffic violation. When asked for his driver's license, the man said he left it at home. However, he did have his social security number—the number on drivers' licenses at the time—and we had his license plate number. The task at hand was to verify his identity.

"Four-two-seven. Driver's license check, please, on SS number one-two-three, four-five, six-seven-eight-nine."

"Four-two-seven. That license number comes out to Soukavong Soutthiphong, date of birth twelve, ten, fifty-five, forty-seven dash one nine nine nine Namoku Street."

My partner's eyes lit up, and a cruel smile appeared on his face. I knew exactly what he was thinking.

"Can you spell that for me. Please."

There was a long pause. You could almost hear the sigh.

"Four-two-seven. Sierra, Oscar, Uniform, Kilo, Alpha, Victor, Oscar, November, Golf. Sierra, Oscar, Uniform, Tango, Tango, Hotel, India, Papa, Hotel, Oscar, November, Golf."

The cruel smile grew and resembled the cunning grin on Dr. Seuss's Grinch.

"Four-two-seven. Dispatch. Can you repeat that?"

Long pause again. "Call me. I'll spell it for you on the phone."

Dispatchers got a lot of abuse.

Most major police departments have, over time, reduced the use of codes in their transmissions. It makes sense. Unless officers and dispatchers are absolutely certain of the codes and lingo, they risk confusing a request or statement. For example,

"Four-two-seven. Ten-seven with four-two-eight at his ten-five on that code thirty-one code ten in that code one. Ten-sixteen the ten-ten, and I'll ten-two for the R.O. and rap check before my ten-fourteen."

It would make so much more sense to simply say, "Four-two-seven. I'm off with Officer four-two-eight on the drunk driver in the stolen car that was involved in the motor vehicle collision. Cancel the ambulance and I'll call you for the registered owner check and rap check on the suspect before I go on my lunch break." The main problem is that sometimes you end up using a lot more words by speaking plainly.

One good thing regarding codes is that in an emergency you don't need to find descriptive words to get your message across. This is most true when you need immediate help.

It was Christmas Day, 1975. I was assigned to Beat 426 on the swing shift. It was about four in the afternoon of a very quiet day. I was wearing a really good-looking wristwatch I had received for Christmas. The call was a normal one.

"Four-two-seven. A report of a code one at Kamehameha Highway and Hawaiian Memorial Park."

"Four-two-seven proceeding."

"Four-two-six proceeding to assist."

We got there fairly quickly and in time to see a very large man punching a smaller man in the face. It seemed that the large man ran the red light and struck the smaller man's car. The large man was also code 25. When we arrived, the large man backed away, and we managed to get the information regarding the collision. When we were finished, we were going to arrest the large man for assault in the third degree and for driving under the influence of alcohol, not to mention a series of citations associated with the collision. After getting all the pertinent info, my partner then told the large man that he was under arrest.

"No, you not." Then he threw a punch at my partner.

We grappled with him briefly and managed to get him to the ground and handcuffed. As we were standing him up, he started shouting for help, calling out the names of other people. We looked down the intersecting street and saw a group of men emerge from a garage. They saw what was happening and called out for even more people. In seconds they were on us. Both my partner and I were being assaulted from every direction. Defensive tactics went out the window. It became a matter of survival.

I pushed away from one man, reached into my car, and grabbed my radio mike.

"Four-two-six, ten-fifteen!" was all I had time to say.

The blows were coming from all angles when I heard sirens coming from the Kailua direction in front of us and from the Kāneʻohe direction behind us. If you're an officer responding to assist another officer who has called for help, you run your siren all the way whether you need it or not. It serves as a notice, as a sign that help is on the way. It also serves as a warning to the offenders that more officers are coming, and perhaps the attack on the victim officer will cease. In our case, all the offenders were pretty drunk, and it took all the officers from Kāneʻohe, Kailua, Kahaluʻu and Waimānalo to break up the group and make arrests. This was another incident that substantiated the notion that HPD is the "biggest gang in town"—in a good way. We can't afford to allow bullies and ruffians to assault people, whether they are citizens or police officers, and get away with it. These suspects were going to be arrested even if our next call was to District One for more backup.

When things settled down, I had a big lump on my left cheek, my jaw hurt big-time, my ribs felt broken, and my badge was missing. We never found it. My blackjack was bent, and we needed three ambulances to care for the arrested men. Eight men were arrested for assault. Another four were arrested for interfering with the duties of a police officer. The rest fled, and we never identified them.

It's a strange thing. The injuries I received in that fight didn't hurt until the fight was over. I didn't feel the strikes and kicks. I felt knocked off balance rather than assaulted. I've been in a fair number of scrapes during my twenty-seven years as an officer, and all of them were that way. The pain of the injury didn't occur until after the fight was over and we were back in control. Then the hurt set in.

The biggest hurt that day was the fact that my new watch was all scratched and broken from being scraped on the roadway.

After being treated at the scene for minor injuries, the suspects were placed into a paddy wagon we requested from District One and transported to Kāne'ohe Station to be booked. We completed our reports, and the maximum bail was set for the suspects. We went home at the end of that night to lick our wounds and heal our pride.

The court case came up a few months later at the Kāne'ohe District Court. The court at that time was part of the Kāne'ohe Police Station. We had extra troops working that day in case anyone became disorderly. Judge Robert Klein—who later served on the Hawai'i Supreme Court—was the judge that day. All twelve suspects were convicted. All twelve suspects were sent to prison for three months. Judge Klein's message was clear. The cases may have been misdemeanor assaults, but you don't assault people; you don't assault police officers.

And as a good officer does, I learned something the day of that assault. When you need help, call for help. There's no shame attached to that. And the HPD system for calling for emergency help works well. A simple code: 10-15.

I also learned not to wear my good watch to work.

12
Kionaole Road

There is a road in Kāneʻohe that is one of the scariest locations on Oʻahu. Not because of imagined ghost stories, but because real tragedies have occurred there. Most of the road is gone now, having been eaten away by the Koʻolau Golf Course and other projects. In the early seventies the road was narrow, overgrown in places, strewn with potholes, and dark even in the daytime. The massive trees along its shoulders grew tall, and branches provided a canopy that hid the sun. Kionaole Road. Its reputation was bad enough for the District Four administration to mandate that officers, particularly the Beat 427 officer, conduct frequent checks of the road twenty-four hours a day.

Kionaole Road branched off Kamehameha Highway near Hawaiian Memorial Park in Kāneʻohe and snaked its way near the base of the Koolaus to where it intersected the old Pali Highway, which people used to traverse the mountain range. Before the Pali tunnels and new highway were built, the old Pali Highway wound down the Koolaus' windward cliffs, and at the base of the mountain just below St. Stephen's Seminary met up with Kionaole Road. Continuing on the old Pali Highway took you to Kailua. Kionaole Road led to Kāneʻohe.

After the new Pali Highway was built and Kamehameha Highway improved, Kionaole Road became a secondary road that serviced the rear of the City and County's Pali Golf Course and a scattering of homes that were clustered at both ends of the road. In addition, there were access roads and trails for the Hawaiian Electric and Hawaiian Telephone companies. What existed between the cluster of homes at each end was overgrown land once used by farmers, many of whom

Kionaole Road, the scariest road on Oʻahu

long ago abandoned their fields. The character of the road changed as its look changed. It became scarier and scarier as it became more and more overgrown, as more and more families left the area and it became more and more deserted. Ghost stories and myths such as those about Hawaiian night marchers added to the scary reputation of the road. But the real-life horrors that occurred there over the years cemented its image as a place you avoided—because if you went there, something bad happened. Two young girls were abducted and taken to Kionaoe, where one was murdered. The other managed to escape. A young woman in college was abducted from Waikīkī, taken to Kionaole, and raped and strangled. Other women reported being raped on Kionaole. A father beat his young son to death and dumped his body on Kionaole. Thieves dumped stolen cars there. Crime happened on Kionaole Road. Violent crime happened on Kionaole Road.

In the seventies, suppressing crime on Kionaole Road required people. Street lighting was not going to come. Roadway improvements were not going to come. New residents were not going to come.

And so we were instructed by our command to provide frequent patrols. It was normally the first thing the Beat 427 officer did each night, check Kionaole Road.

An officer patrolling Kionaole Road should drive slowly, with his blue light on, his windows down, and his air-conditioning and music radio off. That enables him to alert both the crook and the victim that he's coming and to hear a cry for help. A victim lying injured on the side of the road may call out if he sees a car pass.

One night shift I was assigned as the Beat 427 officer. We left our lineup at 2245, and each officer went to his specific beat and made his change-of-shift checks. I went to Kionaole Road. The night was quiet and dark, and the road was deserted. After a few trips around my beat, I stopped at Windy's Drive In at the intersection of Likelike and Kamehameha highways for some coffee. I met another officer there, Bill. Bill was . . . different. And he was fairly new to Kāneʻohe. He loved his coffee, he loved his parrot, which he often took on patrol with him, and he loved to follow other beat officers around. It got so bad at one point that we felt we had a shadow all night long. Bill made no bones about not knowing the windward side of the island at all, and we assumed he followed everyone because he felt lost. We drove around his beat to provide the people who lived there equal protection. And Bill followed us. Everywhere. Except to Kionaole Road. He told us that Kionaole Road was a really bad place and he didn't like driving there.

I sat and enjoyed a cup of coffee with him, and then it was time to go back on the road. To keep him from following me, I mentioned that I was going back to Kionaole Road.

I arrived in a few minutes. About halfway down the road, I came upon a VW Bug parked at the edge of the road. I pulled up behind it and turned on my high beams to illuminate it and the surrounding area. My blue light was on and the windows down. I saw no one. I asked the dispatcher to do a check of the license plates as I waited in the car with the engine running. The dispatcher came back a few minutes later and said that the car was not stolen and was registered to a family who lived in Kailua. I asked the dispatcher to check the telephone book for a phone number. No luck.

"Four-two-seven, please send a Kailua officer to the residence to inquire about the car." I was beginning to suspect that I had found an auto theft. I left my car and walked around the old Bug. The engine was warm, a sign I didn't like. It suggested it had just been dropped off or perhaps the driver was still nearby. I went back to my car and called Bill.

"Four-two-seven to four-two-six."

"Standing by."

"I got a suspicious vehicle on Kionaole. Are you available for backup?"

"Ten-four."

I walked along the edge of the roadway, using my flashlight to see if I could find any sign of someone walking through the grass. My tracking skills weren't that good, and the scruffy grass didn't provide any clues. I heard my number being called by the dispatcher.

"Four-two-seven standing by."

"The owner of the vehicle said her son had the car this morning and went surfing. He was supposed to be home long ago."

"Ten-four. I'll be checking the area." I knew Bill was only a minute away, and after we checked, I would tow the car.

But I really didn't like the sound of things. I didn't know what to make of the situation. This didn't look like an auto theft. The car was in good shape, with the ignition intact. My suspicions began to drift to something much more sinister.

"Four-two-seven . . . four-two-six."

No response. He should have been here by now. Ah, he's probably right around the corner. I left my car to recheck the Bug and surrounding area.

I had walked about twenty yards in front of the Bug when I thought I heard a muffled voice. I turned my flashlight off and stood really still. The headlights of my car illuminated the Bug and surrounding area, and I stood in the light. Then I saw it. Something in the tall elephant grass about twenty yards from the passenger's door was moving toward the car.

Possibilities were flashing in my head. *Someone has a marijuana field. Someone just got murdered. Someone just got raped. Someone just got raped and murdered. And they know my car is there because of my lights. And they know it's a cop. And I don't have a portable radio. And they're between me and my car. Where the hell is Bill?*

I removed my gun from its holster and held it firmly in my right hand. *Where the hell is Bill?*

The elephant grass stopped moving. My heart was racing. I held my gun at a 45-degree angle in front of me, preparing to raise it to firing position. I pocketed my flashlight to free my other hand to hold my gun. *Frickin' Bill.*

The elephant grass moved again to where there was no more elephant grass. The next movement would be someone coming out of the bush. I raised my gun perpendicular to my body and gripped it with both hands now. My finger was on the trigger. I spread my legs to give me balance. *Frickin' Bill.*

It seemed that minutes passed and nothing happened. My arms ached from the unnatural position they were in as they held my several-pound weapon. And then two people stepped from the brush.

"Police! Don't move!"

They spun in my direction. Four hands went above their heads. I could see a young man and a young woman. The guy was half carrying, half dragging a blanket. The young woman started to cry.

I directed the man toward me, giving the woman an opportunity to run, if she was a victim. She followed him. My plan didn't work.

"Both of you, put your hands on the roof of the Volkswagen. And keep them there. You understand?"

"Yes, sir!" came his shaky voice and her tearful one.

I walked up behind them, one eye watching the brush for signs of anyone else. I lowered my gun toward the roadway.

"Are you with him?" I asked, as I tapped the young woman on the shoulder.

The guy answered with a quick "Yes."

"I'm asking her."

She also responded with a tearful "Yes."

"What were you doing in the bushes?"

The guy shook his head with a movement that said, *What are you, an idiot?*

The young woman started to cry again. "Are you going to call our parents?" she asked.

Why the hell do young lovers pick the most out-of-the-way places? The moment I thought about that question, I realized the answer.

I then asked for IDs. Both kids were eighteen and therefore out of my jurisdiction. Both were scared, and I realized I had a hand in that. My voice calmed quite a bit as I lectured them on the hazards of Kionaole Road and going into the brush as they did. The young woman stopped crying, and they both agreed their actions were dangerous.

I told the man that I would have another officer notify his parents that we found him and that he was okay. And that was all I was going to report. Satisfied that all I found were two young lovers who made a bad choice of places to be alone, I released them with a "stay away from Kionaole Road." I could think of only one thing as I got back in my car and watched the VW Bug drive off.

Frickin' Bill.

• • • • •

Those of us who enter the field of law enforcement realize that there is some danger associated with that career. We understand that we can get hurt. At times we actually do get hurt. We do everything we can to minimize those situations, but sometimes they're completely out of our control. We follow our training, we follow our heads, we follow our hearts, and most of the time we're okay.

With the understanding that we can get hurt in police work comes a commitment to serve in spite of and often in the face of the possibility of injury. This is one of the reasons I have emphasized to my students that police work is not a solo job. Much of what an officer does is done as part of a team, whether that team includes an officer and his beat partner, his sector, his watch, or his district.

Two officers may dislike each other, but when needs arise, each officer puts that dislike aside and responds to the needs of his fellow officer. He or she would expect it from me, and I expect it from them. When an officer needs help from another officer, that officer must respond—with safety and caution, of course. It serves no purpose to the officer or civilian needing help if the responding officer is hurt and cannot assist.

When Bill chose not to respond to my request for assistance on Kionaole Road, he violated this basic principle of helping his fellow officer. I didn't say anything to him, but I was angry and disappointed and I discussed this with some of my fellow beat officers. We all agreed that Bill needed to know that this was unacceptable. We also agreed that he needed to feel what it's like to be alone in an unpleasant situation. The sinister, conniving minds of our sector pulled together and came up with a plan to teach Bill a lesson. Naturally, we did not involve our sector sergeant in this. We wanted to keep him out of trouble by allowing him his "plausible deniability." He wouldn't have allowed us to pull this stunt anyway.

So one day after lineup, we all stood around talking just outside the station and someone suggested that we go out to Kionaole Road and see if it was true about the Hawaiian night marchers. It was rumored that on a dark night you could see the shadows of long-dead Hawaiian warriors who were thrown off the Pali by Kamehameha I's warriors. These shadows of the dead would travel to the sea in a long line from the brush at the foot of the mountain where they died. Or at least that's what we suggested to Bill. It was sort of a warm-up for what was to come a little later. Initially Bill didn't want to go. He had things to check on his beat. No, no, no, we protested. This is a sector project. Everybody goes. But he had his parrot that night. No, no, no, we repeated. This is a sector project. Everybody goes. We insisted. In fact there were some of us in front of him and some of us behind him. He came with us, but reluctantly.

We entered Kionaole at the Kāneʻohe end and slowly wound our way to the Pali end, where the road made large U-turns, enabling us to park our cars in one spot. With our lights off, we got out and shared some coffee from a thermos and began telling ghost stories. The night was very quiet, enabling all of us to participate in this lesson of responsibility. We also bribed the dispatcher with food not to bother us unless it was necessary. We told all the ghost stories we knew. Being in the dark on Kionaole with the night chill turning colder and the rustling branches, leaves, and grasses providing a surreal background, it was fairly easy to raise a goose bump or two.

One of the stories was that of an old man who became despondent and went out to a tree on Kionaole, climbed high off the ground and hung himself. They say he slowly strangled. He kicked his legs and tried to pull himself up with his arms because he changed his mind about killing himself, but it was too late, and his life was slowly choked out of him until his twitching body came to rest. And since then, his ghost would come back and hang again from that tree, and unsuspecting cars would turn the corner and there he was, hanging from the tree in the road in front of them.

"That's right," came one response. "I knew a guy who saw him hanging before he was cut down."

"That's nothing," came another. "My uncle was with the fire department and was one of the guys who cut him down."

"And if you look into the tree, you can still see the rope hanging from the branch to where it was cut by the firemen."

"Nah!"

"Yes, you can. In fact, the tree is right around the corner."

Well, that was enough for the group to agree to go take a look. Bill followed us. We reached the tree, a large, beautiful monkeypod. Its wide canopy of branches covered the road and blotted out the night sky. Fingers of roots reached downward, stretching toward the earth to form even greater support to the branches overhead.

Even though we were a group, the dark, the tree, the locale—everything—gave us all goose bumps.

"Hey, Bill, this is where we tie you to the tree and leave you until morning."

"What?"

We told him how we felt about his displays of fear. We told him that as police officers we all go to help one another when there's need. We told him that his behavior hurt all of us. Bill looked embarrassed. He explained that he didn't like working in the country and that he already put in his transfer request.

Fair enough. But while he was going to be with us, he needed to be one of us. He said he understood, and to the best of my knowledge, did his part until he left.

13
A Good Laugh

Our watch in District Four was renowned for the frequent pranks we pulled on one another. Most of us participated in one prank or another, but the king of pranksters during the time I was in D-4 was Tony. Tony would not miss an opportunity to pull a good one when he could, and that practice rubbed off on the rest of us. This helped reduce the stress of the job. Too many times we worked short-handed, and a harmless joke helped ease that stress. You must understand that none of us allowed any joke to get in the way of the task at hand, and we never ever placed another person at risk. At least we tried not to place our buddies at risk, but sometimes it backfired. Most of the pranks were pulled at night when it was easier to scare someone.

It was around two or three in the morning. Kāneʻohe was asleep. The alarm call came in that there was a possible entry at the Ulu Mau Village restaurant in Heʻeia Kea. We all responded. "All" on that night meant only three of us. Many a night there were only three officers working from Pali Highway to Chinaman's Hat. Since we were coming from a long distance away, we had to speed with blue lights flashing to get there quickly. On this night, I got there last. Tony and Alan were already out of their cars. I got out and started walking quickly up the plant-covered walkway. Suddenly, a voice came from the bushes.

"Hello, Gary," was all he said.

I dropped my flashlight as I spun, but my gun was already on its way out of its holster.

"Hey, hey, it's me," Tony said from the plants.

"Son of a bitch! You scared the shit out of me," I said, reholstering my weapon.

"Gotcha," he grinned, and we walked the rest of the way to the restaurant.

"Where's Alan?"

"I dunno. He was here before I got here."

BANG! Both of our guns were out of our holsters as we ran up to the building. Tony pointed for me to go left, and he went right. As I worked my way around the side of the building, my eyes searching for a possible break-in, I ran the sound of the explosion again and again through my head. It didn't sound like our guns. Perhaps it wasn't Alan who fired. Perhaps someone shot at Alan. Perhaps Alan was shot. But something about that explosion was wrong.

I turned the corner to the back of the restaurant and saw Tony at the other corner. We could both see an open door. The room inside was dark except for the quickly moving beam of a flashlight.

We decided it was time. Tony shouted out, "Alan!"

"In here," came his response.

Not good enough for us. We both remained at our positions, which in hindsight were poor ones. Tony and I were facing each other—not where we wanted to be if we had to fire our weapons.

"You okay?"

"Yeah, yeah. Come inside."

We still didn't move.

"You fired your gun?"

"No. I threw a pot at a rat. Come inside."

The joke was on Tony and me. And one wasn't even played.

Sometimes things happen and we just shake our heads and try not to feel too foolish. One day we got a call that a patient from the Hawai'i State Hospital had escaped. In hospital jargon it's called "elopement." I was just around the corner from the hospital when the call came in. Driving up the road to the buildings, I saw a man walking down the path. As I got closer I saw that he was a Caucasian man in his forties with a graying handlebar mustache. He was wearing a white shirt, long pants, and shoes. I pulled alongside him.

"Excuse me, are you from the hospital?"

Hawai'i State Hospital

"Yes, I'm Dr. Johanson. I was walking down here trying to locate the missing patient."

"Doctor, what building is he from?"

He directed me to a building up the hill. I thanked him and drove up. When I arrived, I met with one of the nurses, who explained that one of the patients just walked off, a few minutes before I arrived.

"Yes, I spoke to Dr. Johanson on the way up."

"Haole guy? Handlebar mustache?"

"Yeah." I knew what was coming next.

"That was the patient."

I went back to my car muttering that they should have given a description when they called. The nurse was laughing and shaking her head as I left. The guy was gone.

The Hawai'i State Hospital was famous for runaway patients. During another incident, several of us responded to an elopement and were checking an abandoned building to see if the person was hiding there. It was routine already. We were walking through the barrackslike building, which was empty and uninhabited. As we approached the far side, we neared a series of toilet stalls. Isaac was nearest the row of toilets and was bouncing the doors open as we passed. He bounced the last one and immediately stumbled away from the stall, sprawling across the floor. There, sitting on the toilet, was the escapee, his pants down around his ankles.

"Damn, I just using the bathroom. You guys gotta kick my door in?"

Sometimes the perpetrator of the joke wasn't even human. I responded to a domestic argument in Kāneʻohe. When I arrived, the husband of the complainant was already gone. She invited me in to give her side of the story, and as soon as I entered the house, the smallest Chihuahua I ever saw ran up and bit me on the ankle through my sock. The woman shooed him out of the house and I took her statement, every now and again rubbing the twinge on my leg. I completed the statement and asked her to call me back when her husband returned so I could speak to him. As I left, the little dog ran up from behind and bit me on the back of my calf. As if he expected to be stepped on, he attacked and ran away. The woman was apologetic, but I advised her to control her dog before he bit someone else—maybe a child. She explained that she didn't know what got into Jesus, because he was normally the best little dog.

Jesus? Pronounced "Hey-soos" by the woman. It was because he was such a good little dog, she said, reading my puzzled face.

I got into my car and was about to close the door when Jesus came up and bit me a third time on the leg. I tried to crush his little head in my door frame, but the little creep was too fast and took off running.

One event that had absolutely no humor at the time it happened was funny in a slapstick sort of way when we looked back on it. Actually, it was funny and sad at the same time. It was funny because of how the event evolved, but sad since it ended with a marriage breaking up.

Our evening shift was over, and a group of us decided to go to the Tiki Tops Bar in the Windward City Shopping Center. One young officer had a complicated arrangement. He was married, but was also seeing two young women at the same time. That night, he met us at Tiki Tops for a beer with one of the women. Unfortunately, the second woman he was seeing had the bright idea to check Tiki Tops, where she knew we sometimes went after work. His car was there, so she parked and walked in.

Three, maybe four seconds passed before the screaming started. The third unfortunate thing then occurred. His wife, who knew he was at the bar because he told her, and who decided to join him for a beer, walked in the door. Everything went quiet for a heartbeat. Then the proverbial "all hell broke loose." Fists, ashtrays, beer bottles went flying, mostly in the direction of the unfortunate officer.

The rest of us quickly retreated to the safety of our cars and sped out of the parking lot. We figured that it would be only minutes before the night shift officers arrived, and it would be in our best interests not to be present when they did. The next day, and for several days after, we listened to lectures about ethical behavior during off-duty time, creating disturbances in bars when we are the people who usually break those things up, etc. And we needed those lectures. It took a long time, and we all felt bad about what happened, but we eventually did laugh about that wild night at the Tiki Tops Bar.

There are times when officers are placed in situations in which ethical behavior balances on a fence, so to speak. The position, the uniform, the gun all have an effect on some women. Usually it's younger women who are infatuated with the image. They're called groupies. And some officers take advantage of them. They see themselves as readily available studs on the prowl for their next available woman. And that was more true in the late seventies, when people still talked about a sexual revolution, no one had heard of AIDS, and people drank a lot more.

A sergeant who worked in Waikīkī frequently bragged that the only reason he worked there was to meet and sleep with as many different women as possible. He shared his tales of sexual adventures with the young officers, some of whom gazed at him with wide eyes, wondering if they would ever attain his sexual prowess. One night he explained that all he had to do in the course of his eight-hour day was ask ten female tourists if they wanted to get laid. Inevitably, he boasted, one out of the ten would be interested. And he didn't even need to find a room. I held my opinion to myself, but I thought all along that this sergeant was really full of hot air.

But sometimes tourists, both men and women, actively sought a temporary relationship while visiting Waikīkī. One night years later, when I was a new detective, I was assigned to investigate an attempted murder on Kalākaua Avenue. Two people got into an argument, and one drove his car onto the sidewalk, striking the second. One of the witnesses was a woman visiting from California. The beat officers took her preliminary statement, but when I arrived on the scene, she stated that she couldn't talk to me right then because she had an early flight home in the morning and wanted to start packing. I explained that I needed a more detailed statement, and she asked that I come to her room in a nearby hotel in about an hour. I did, and when I arrived she opened the door and began filling in the missing pieces of her original statement. She walked into the bathroom as she was speaking and moments later walked out nude.

"You know," she said, "I've been here seven days and I have yet to get laid. I'm leaving tomorrow morning and I really don't want to be disappointed."

The guys back at the station didn't believe me. Some didn't believe that I would be so foolish as to turn down such an offer; others didn't believe the story at all.

I just hope the woman wasn't too disappointed with her Hawai'i vacation, but it was obvious she didn't run into our conquistador sergeant.

All kinds of weird and funny things happen in police work, and sometimes you have to draw the line. But I just don't think Jesus should be the name of a dog.

14
When Officers Need Help

Police departments today recognize signs warning that an officer is suffering a great deal of stress. Often, these indicators are tied to everyday life and may seem normal on the surface. Great debt is one indicator. It's easy for a young officer struggling to create a good life for himself and his family to get way over his head in debt.

A much more common indicator of too much stress in an officer's life is alcohol abuse. It is not uncommon for officers to gather regularly at a bar after work to "unwind." It becomes a problem when these meetings become more and more frequent and the unwinding in a bar becomes a need. And sometimes a single officer drinks to excess nearly every day. Officer Stan was such an officer. He was one of the nicest people you would like to know, except for his drinking problem. Because of it, he often got into trouble at work and was disciplined for various things, all due to his drinking. When he arrived at work smelling of alcohol, our sergeant sent him home, which created a staffing problem that affected the rest of us. There were times when we couldn't smell the alcohol, but he was suffering its effects and would fall asleep and be disciplined for it.

In spite of his problem, we couldn't help feeling sorry for him, because things happened to him that made his life difficult. One day, for example, when Stan was on the beat in Lāʻie, he took his dog with him, a German shepherd named Duchess. Three of us stopped in the shade of a building at Lāʻie Elementary School to chit-chat for a while, and the talk eventually focused on Stan's dog. She was a friendly dog, Stan said, and very obedient. We were worried that the dog might scare someone, but Stan insisted that she was vary tame and let her out of the car to show us. Duchess jumped out of the backseat and immediately ran across the huge lawn of the school. And kept running. And kept running. Stan ran after her, shouting "Duchess! Duchess!" But the dog paid him no mind and disappeared among the houses behind Lāʻie Elementary School. Stan drove and drove around the neighborhoods looking for Duchess. We helped look, but we never found her. We could clearly see that the loss of this dog hurt him.

His alcohol problems didn't seem to get any better, and the supervisors were getting on him because of it. He was more and more grouchy and came to work smelling of alcohol more frequently. One night Stan and I were assigned to Waimānalo. I couldn't tell just how under the weather he was, but it was apparent that he had been drinking sometime earlier in the evening. Our watch hit the road, and I decided to check on the sentries at Bellows Air Force Base. We had a good relationship with the military there, and we sometimes took them coffee and vice versa. When I arrived, Stan was already there. We talked to the sentries, discussing the crime problems they were having on base and trying to see if there was any correlation between their problems and crimes in the community. Stan looked tired, and he said he was having a difficult time remaining awake just sitting and talking. He decided to roll his windows down and cruise Waimānalo to wake up. I told him to come back and park if he found he couldn't stay awake.

I heard nothing from Stan and assumed he was all right. After a while, I drove out myself and patrolled my beat, drifting into Enchanted Lake on one end and Sandy Beach at the other. The night was moving on, and there was still no sign of Stan. I wondered if he went home. Probably not. Perhaps he fell asleep somewhere. I checked all the major roads, stores, and parking lots. I called him once.

"Four-two-oh to four-two-one."

There was no answer. I didn't want to get him in trouble with our sergeant by repeatedly calling him on the radio with no answer, so I went back to Bellows and parked with the sentries. They hadn't seen him since he left a few hours ago.

After some time passed, I heard sirens in the distance. They sounded like HFD, and shortly after they went on, the Kāne'ohe dispatcher put out a call for Stan and me to respond to Waimānalo Elementary School on a possible fire. Stan didn't respond that he was proceeding. As soon as I turned the bend in the road and hit the stretch that led to the school, I could see the glow of the flames. I notified dispatch that there actually was a fire at the old wooden school. HFD was already there hooking up hoses. One of the firemen was waving at me and directing me toward the area of the fire. I pulled onto the grass, and as I turned the corner of one building I saw Stan's car parked next to the burning building. Firefighters were alternately shooting down his car and the building with water. I ran to his car. Stan was fast asleep. A firefighter told me they were going to break his rear window. I yelled to them to give me one minute and began shouting into the rolled-up window of his car. He jerked awake and moved his car out of the way of the firefighters, who extinguished the fire.

Stan admitted to our sergeant that he was absolutely wrong. He accepted his discipline. But nothing was done to help him. In the early seventies, we didn't think the department should take a more proactive role with officers who suffered personal problems that affected their behavior. We thought that officers like Stan should have been more responsible for their own actions. We were wrong. The rest of us should have been more responsible for Stan's behavior and the behavior of officers like him. Instead of feeling sorry for Stan and not wanting him to get in trouble, we should have been taking steps to get help for him.

I don't know what happened to Stan. After I got promoted and left District Four, I lost track of him. I heard he eventually quit the department, long before he was eligible to retire.

Sometimes intervention programs simply don't reach the person in trouble. Isaac, the same officer pushing open the toilet-stall doors at the Hawai'i State Hospital, was one of our senior officers in Kāne'ohe. He had been in the department for some time, and we younger officers turned to him for advice. He was an easygoing man who seemed destined for higher rank within the department. In fact, Isaac was eventually promoted to the rank of captain. One day Isaac met Marie and they fell in love. Marie was a dispatcher with HPD, and they clicked. Everything seemed right and their marriage worked well. Sadly, Marie was diagnosed with cancer, and after a long illness, died. Isaac was devastated. One day, his grief was too much to bear anymore, and Isaac ended his life, one he didn't want to live without his Marie.

We'll never know if intervention by the department would have changed things in Isaac's case, but his wasn't the first or the last suicide by an officer who believed his depression was too difficult to bear. It is comforting to know, however, that our department has grown to understand that it is their leaders' responsibility to recognize the warning signs of stress or depression, and to act on them.

Today, nearly every large organization, including police agencies, has Employee Assistance Programs to help employees through problems such as alcohol abuse and depression. A police psychologist is available to all employees, and a crisis intervention peer group responds to traumatic incidents to offer services at the scene if officers need help. Education about and awareness of the effects of stress have led officers to accept the fact that in spite of their seemingly invincible facade, they are susceptible to the effects of stress and the traumatic incidents that sometimes explode into the lives of police officers. We have come to realize that stress is cumulative. It doesn't require a life-threatening incident for an officer to need assistance. Just the day-to-day routines of a beat officer's life are stressful. Unless addressed, this cumulative stress can lead to burnout, and a once-productive officer's career can be dramatically affected. Thankfully, HPD's leaders eventually realized this and provided their officers programs to help them through difficult times.

15
An Umbrella and a Stolen Car

It was raining. No, it was storming. Pouring cats and dogs. We were on the midnight shift and no one was on the road. I was assigned to Waimānalo, but I don't remember who my beat partner was that night. We were parked at Bellows Air Station waiting for the thunderstorm to pass. Occasionally, one of us checked the highway for anyone who might need help. We did this for a couple of hours. The rain didn't let up. After a while, my beat partner said he needed to make a 10-1, return to Kailua Station. About twenty minutes later, the dispatcher sent two of the Kailua beat officers to the Kapaʻa Quarry Road on a possible rape in progress.

When "in progress" offenses are reported, the primary officers respond to the scene, and other officers in the surrounding area take up posts in the event the suspect flees in their direction. Too often, inexperienced beat officers all rush to the scene. Take a bank robbery for example. The robber goes in and demands money, the teller gives him some money and sets off a robbery alarm. The alarm company gets the electronic alert and calls HPD, passing the information to the Communications Division call taker, who relays this to the dispatcher, who in turn dispatches an officer. The entire process may take as long as a minute. Normally, officers take about three minutes to arrive at a scene. Add to this the initial delays, and by the time the first officer arrives, the suspect has been gone at least four minutes. This could put the suspect miles away. If all the officers responded to the scene of the offense, we would never catch anyone.

So I waited at the entrance to Bellows on Kalanianaʻole Highway with my lights off and engine running for any additional information on the case. The initial officers called that they were 10-7, arrived at the scene. Soon after they reported that, a guard for HC & D observed a car parked near their property, and when he went to check, he heard a woman screaming for help. He approached the car and saw two men and a woman. The woman was nude. She screamed that she had been raped and that the men had a gun. One of the men pointed a gun at the guard, and they quickly drove off in the direction of the Pali Highway. The guard didn't get a license plate number, but he described the car as a big, white Oldsmobile.

Shortly after the additional information came over the air, a big white Oldsmobile with three people in the front drove by me, headed in the Makapu'u direction. It was still raining hard. I turned my headlights on and pulled out behind the car. I notified dispatch that I had a car matching the description with what appeared to be two males with one woman sitting between them in the front seat. The Olds slowed down to about fifteen miles per hour, and before the dispatcher could come back with a registered-owner check, the car pulled off to the side of the road. I pulled off behind it. I turned on my blue light, but I stayed in my car, knowing that other officers were on the way to my location.

Suddenly, there was a commotion in the front seat of the Oldsmobile. The woman appeared to be trying to get out. The passenger door flew open, and a nude woman jumped from the car and began running toward my car. She was screaming, "He's got a gun." As I was getting out of my car, she shouted again that he had a gun. I drew mine out of my holster. She got into my passenger seat. It was still raining hard. I shouted at the driver to get out of the car. My eyes moved from driver's door to passenger's door. My gun followed the movement of my eyes, but the rain was making it hard to see. Slowly the driver got out and raised his hands over his head. I ordered him to lie on the ground. He immediately complied. I pointed my gun at him as he lowered himself to the ground. Sergeant Frank Sua had told us that you never show 'em that you're "a little bit scared." The reality was that I was a heck-of-a-lot scared.

I shouted to the passenger to get out. He didn't move. It was still raining very hard. I shouted at him again to obey my orders. He reached into the backseat and fumbled with something. My heart was racing. I shouted at the man lying on the roadway.

"Driver, stay on the ground."

The passenger door swung open. The passenger swung his legs out. He quickly got out of the car and turned to face me. That's when I saw him carrying it at port arms position. My mind screamed RIFLE! I swung my gun toward him. Suddenly his arms jerked. I fired. BOOM! The flash from the muzzle of my firearm blinded me for just an instant.

The man started screaming something I couldn't understand as he opened the umbrella he was holding like a rifle in his hands. A damn umbrella. The woman in my car was screaming again. I was screaming, "Don't f—king move." The guy lying on the road was stiff as a tree, his fingers, hands, arms, and feet stretching away from his body as if he were a flying squirrel. I ordered the passenger to come around the car and get down on the ground. He didn't seem to be worried about getting wet anymore and threw the umbrella down. In less than a minute, other officers were on the scene and both suspects were in handcuffs.

The two suspects were marines from the Kāneʻohe Marine Corps base. The woman said she had been drinking with them in Kailua and they said they were going to take her home. Instead, they took her to Kapaʻa Quarry Road and raped her. We found a small handgun under the driver's seat.

As for me, I was having a panic attack from having fired my weapon. I thanked God that I only fired once and missed. I could have injured or killed him. I knew I had discharged my firearm in violation of our rules. You see, all during recruit school, and even while on the beat, it was drummed into our heads that if we drew our weapons, we shot to kill. The reason we shot to kill was that someone was using deadly force against us. If that condition didn't exist, we did not draw our firearms. Period. Honolulu police officers don't shoot people. In this instance, however, I would have been completely justified.

I felt sick. We were back at the Kailua Station. The woman was given some clothes and a blanket, the two suspects were booked and sitting in the holding cells, and the detective who was handling the case was speaking to my sergeant. I felt like throwing up. You see, up to that point, I had said nothing about firing my weapon. That's how panicked I was. I finally realized I could keep quiet no longer. I pulled my sergeant aside and told him the truth. I remember that he had a compassionate look on his face, a look that said, *You really screwed this one up, kid; it was nice knowing ya.* He told me to just sit there and wait, and went back to the detective. They disappeared into the sergeant's office. Other officers began looking at me like, *What did you do?* But I said nothing. After what seemed like an age, the sergeant and detective came out, and they both glanced at me. The detective walked away, and the sergeant motioned me to him. We went inside the sergeant's office. He closed the door, opened a drawer of the file cabinet, and brought out a gun cleaning kit.

"Clean your gun. And I don't want to hear anymore about how your gun went off accidentally out there. And I don't ever want to hear that you discussed this with anyone else."

He walked out of the room before I could say anything or ask any questions. I cleaned my firearm as well as it has ever been cleaned. And I never discussed that Waimānalo incident with anyone. Years later, another incident involving a very real rifle would occur in Kaka'ako, and again the notion that Honolulu police officers don't shoot people nearly cost us our lives.

● ● ● ● ●

I had to have one. My car was ugly. My car was slow. My car didn't have a good sound system. My car didn't have air-conditioning. Everyone else had one. Why couldn't I? So one day I went back to

Aloha Motors and traded my Chevelle for an Oldsmobile Cutlass Supreme. Okay, so it only had a V-6. Okay, so it only had an AM-FM-tape system. But it had power windows and air. And class. My Olds Cutlass Supreme. Navy blue, with black faux leather seats. And matching colored rims, with big wide tires. I was driving in style.

One day while driving in style, I was cruising the grounds of the Hawai'i State Hospital and pulled behind an old Plymouth Valiant. The driver looked really nervous, so I ran a license check.

"Dispatch, four-two-eight, the vehicle is reported stolen."

My blood pressure soared. Since my first day on the beat, I had never managed to catch a stolen vehicle with the driver inside. I gave my location, and at least three of my beat partners radioed that they were proceeding toward me. I followed the Valiant slowly, waiting for the other officers to arrive, but I guess the driver got nervous, because he punched it into high gear. The Valiant took off with me in pursuit, my blue light flashing and my siren screaming. As I chased, I gave details.

"He's running . . . turning left on Kahekili . . . turning right on Kahuhipa . . . turning right on Kam."

I continued to give my direction and cross streets so my beat partners could plan their approach. This was the seventies. The department did not have a policy on high-speed chases as it does today, so my attitude was simple. *You are NOT going to get away from me!*

I maintained a safe distance behind him, my siren actually help-ing to clear the road for the speeding car. He ran red lights as he sped through Kāne'ohe town in the Kailua direction. As we approached the major intersection of Kamehameha and Likelike highways, the light was red for us, and the traffic was moving mauka on Likelike. Without slowing, the stolen car turned directly into the path of a city bus. I watched the bus dip wildly as the driver hit the brakes to avoid hitting the Valiant. I envisioned the standing passengers flying for-ward, perhaps injuring themselves. The Valiant hit the bus's right bumper. The scraping collision didn't have any effect. The Valiant continued up Likelike. I had to climb the grassy shoulder to avoid hitting the bus myself.

I continued to chase the Valiant up Likelike. It was here that I felt my first disappointment with my new Cutlass Supreme. My little V-6 was no match for the big Plymouth V-8 that was obviously under the Valiant's hood. I once owned a '64 Valiant that had a big V-8, and I knew firsthand how that little car could move. I knew there was no way my little V-6 was going to catch him.

"Tony," I called, ignoring the protocol of using call numbers, "he's pulling away from me. We need you up front."

Tony had the fastest car in the district, and I knew that once Tony got up front, we would not lose the auto thief.

"I'm coming," came Tony's response.

Three-quarters of the way up Likelike, Tony passed me. We sped through the tunnel, and the Valiant collided with two other cars as he changed lanes. Going downhill on the Honolulu side of Likelike was a lot easier on my engine, and I was able to catch up with Tony and the crook. As we neared the bottom of Likelike at the intersection of Kula Kolea Street, I said to myself, *We got him!* I could see officers from the Kalihi District waiting for us, and traffic was backed up at the light in three of the four lanes. The left-turn lane was blocked. The two middle lanes were blocked, and the right-turn lane was coned off by street workers who were repainting the lines at the intersection.

But that didn't slow the car thief. He slammed into the rears of two cars in the middle lanes, forcing himself between them. Tony hit his brakes hard, and his car spun sideways. I turned right, into the coned-off lane, sending cones flying. In my peripheral vision, I could see the street workers sprinting to get out of my way. I managed to get through the intersection without hitting anything, or anyone, except traffic cones. Now I was following an officer from the Kalihi District who was right behind the suspect. We sped down Likelike and onto Kamehameha IV Road, sirens screaming.

Suddenly, the officer in front of me extended his left arm out his window. I could see he had his gun in his hand. I heard three pops, and I remember thinking, *Oh great. Just what I need, somebody sending bullets into a residential area.*

We sped off Kamehameha IV and onto Middle Street. Suddenly, the Valiant turned onto a small side street. We followed. I was completely lost in a few seconds as the Valiant turned onto this road and that lane trying to lose us. And then he made a mistake. He turned onto a dead-end gravel road. He hit his brakes and slid to a stop. The officer behind him was stopping. I hit my brakes. They were gone—they must have overheated. I dropped my gear shift to first, but it didn't help. The suspect was getting out of his car when I slammed into the rear of the car in front of me. That car slammed into the Valiant, pushing it through an old tile wall and causing it to come to rest against a house. The suspect was bounced around in the collision and fell down. The cop in front of me and I were on the suspect like the proverbial flies on . . . you know what. After the suspect was cuffed, the Kalihi cop turned to me.

"What! You couldn't stop? My car's brand new!"

"No brakes. And mine's new, too."

That was no consolation for him. He roughly brought the suspect to his feet and gave me an angry stare. "This is my arrest!"

That was fine with me. I felt bad about damaging his car—and mine. I also felt bad that I started a chase that created a series of traffic accidents (now called "traffic collisions"). In addition, a large local woman came out of the damaged house, screaming, "Who's goin' pay for dis?"

We booked the suspect at the District One receiving desk, and I typed my follow-up report. The Kalihi cop refused to speak to me. Although I was sorry about his car, I was beginning to feel indignant at him for firing bullets at the moving car under the circumstances we were in. That was and still is against our rules. As I walked out of the squad room, I walked up to him and apologized again and added that he shouldn't have shot at the fleeing car. He didn't say anything. I wondered if he worried that I was going to turn him in. I didn't.

A day or so later, my major called me into his office before lineup.

"The total damage estimate for all the collisions in that wild chase was over forty-five thousand dollars."

I thought he was going to say it was going to come out of my pay a little at a time. I don't know for sure, but this chase was probably one of the many that forced the department to put limits on high-speed chases. The policy now calls for greater restraint. We can't chase in order to issue a traffic tag anymore. And for good reason. When an officer chases a suspect who refuses to stop, he is just acting as an accelerant for that vehicle, pushing it faster and faster. Officers are authorized to *follow* rather than chase. When does chase become follow and vice versa? I don't know, but beat sergeants have the responsibility to call off a chase if it appears to be getting out of control—or when the chase endangers innocent people. The fact is, most high-speed chases occur over misdemeanor offenses during which the suspect refuses to stop.

A few days after that brief meeting with the major, I was assigned to transport the District Four papers to District One headquarters. As I passed Kula Kolea, I noticed a white squiggly line that ran helter-skelter from the right-turn lane onto the sidewalk and into the grassy shoulder where a street worker pushed his paint dispenser trying desperately to get out of my way a few days before.

It took a long time for the squiggly lines of paint to fade away.

16
Promotion

The Honolulu Police Department is about as bureaucratic as an agency can get. The department, like all bureaucracies, has a great number of rules and regulations that define how the agency is to be run, who is to do what, and exactly how is it to be done. From time to time, the department has streamlined its operations, but with little effect. While I was a member of the department, there were General Orders, Special Orders, Administrative Notices, Departmental Manuals of Operations, and God knows what else. Put all the folders together and they would extend about five feet.

The department was forced to make changes in the way it presented its rules and regulations when a reporter asked for a particular procedure and the request was refused. After a threat of civil suit and a review by the city attorneys, a new method of documentation became the rule. Now there are simply Policies and Procedures. If I'm not mistaken, policies, but not the procedures, may be reviewed by the media—the policy being "what" the rule is and the procedure telling how to do it. Same thing, different package. At least there's a rule now that tells what a reporter may and may not look at.

But back in 1976, the number of rules and regulations was tremendous. Fortunately, it wasn't as important for a particular officer to know every rule and procedure as it was for him to know how and where to quickly find them. Except on exams. On exams, he really did need to know every rule and procedure, because there was a specific section of the test devoted to "rules and regs."

I had been with the department for over four years when I became eligible to take the exam for promotion to sergeant. Because I had more than two years of college credit, I was allowed to take the exam before the end of the usual five-year waiting period. It was a perk the department was offering as enticement for officers to obtain college degrees. (Much later in my career, it became apparent that to progress beyond the ranks of lieutenant and captain, I would need a bachelor's degree. That spurred me on to complete the college courses I abandoned in 1971.)

When the exam was announced, I initially thought I didn't have enough time in the department to seek promotion. Many, many officers on the force had more experience than I. But since the department was pushing for me to take the exam, I did.

A civil service exam is not difficult. The answers are multiple choice or true-false. The difficulty is in the preparation. The level of preparation is as varied among officers as the officers themselves. Some don't prepare at all. This group usually grumbles the loudest at their low scores and their failure to ever get promoted. They say the department isn't being fair in giving such difficult exams. At the other extreme are those who overprepare. They memorize every rule and regulation, every penal code, every self-help promotional exam book they can get their hands on, and compile lists of questions remembered by officers who took the exam the year before.

The most difficult part may have been applying to take the exam. I think my experience was pretty typical. First I had to fill out an application. Then I had to submit my college transcript or diploma to prove I had the necessary college credits, even though those credits were already on file with City and County Civil Service because I submitted them when I first applied for the job. Now, however, they needed to see a fresh copy—as if the original copy had depreciated. I also had to show proof from HPD Personnel Division that I had the experience necessary to obtain the points that made me eligible to take the exam in the first place. Didn't Civil Service have a record that I was a civil servant? I applied with them when I was first seeking employment. Did they not keep record of that? Why did they demand proof that I worked for over four years with the department that they hired me to? The answer to this question is "bureaucracy and bureaucrats." When you ask a civil service worker the same question, however, the answer you get is, "It's the rules." When you hear politicians say they want to reform civil service, vote for them.

So I went through the process of applying to take the promotional exam. Succeeding in that without grabbing a civil service clerk by the throat should by itself have made me eligible for instant promotion. Some time later, in the mail, I got a card telling me that I was eligible to take the test and that another card would come later telling me where to take the test. Say, wouldn't combining those two cards save work, paper, and postage? Wait, I know, "It's the rules." So I waited and got another card notifying me to report to the Farrington High School Cafeteria on a particular day. But I worked on that day. Could I swap to the other exam on a different day at the McKinley High School cafeteria? No? Okay, I understand, "It's the rules."

So I took a day of vacation and reported to the Farrington High School cafeteria. I turned in my admission card and was assigned a seat. Seats were spaced five feet apart, just to remove the opportunity to cheat. What! Us cheat? You betcha. Keep that guy five feet away from me; I don't want him looking at my answer sheet. (Actually, if we're caught cheating on a promotional exam, we're barred from eligibility for that exam and the next one, three years later. We went to the bathroom before we went in and got our seats, too. 'Cause if we had to go pee during the test, everybody knew we went to our cars to look up an answer.) The answer sheet was passed out upside down. We couldn't even look at that until the proctor told us it was time. It's the rules. More rules were explained, and we were allowed to look at our answer sheets and write our names on them. Then came the exam packet. The exam itself was inside a pamphlet that had a cover sheet and additional instructions. It too was passed out upside down. It's the . . . well, you know.

"You may not begin until I say *begin*," the proctor informed the group.

There was a long silence as he looked around the room at everyone. Then he straightened up tall and performed his civil servant responsibility.

"Begin."

Pages ruffled and exam takers flipped through the exam book looking for the sections they hoped would not be there. Alas, the section on rules and regs was included in this exam, just as it was in all the exams that came before. The proctor and his assistants walked among the tables and benches, deliberately trying to make us uncomfortable.

The exam was designed to take three hours to complete. At forty-five minutes into the exam, an officer I didn't know stood up, threw his pencils across the room, shouted, "To hell with this!" and walked out. The proctor calmly walked over to the empty seat and with an ever-so-slight smile, retrieved the papers with a look that said, *Victim number one.*

I thought some sections were easy and some very hard. I came away thinking that I passed, but perhaps not with a high score. Oh, well, next time.

About four weeks later another card came in the mail. I scored well after all. I was ranked in position number seven. That was certainly delightful, but unexpected. I lucked out in taking the exam when I did, since ours was the last promotional exam in which we were ranked solely on our college credit, experience, and exam results. Every exam after ours also required an interview.

A month or so passed, but the big day finally came. I was notified to report to District One headquarters, second-floor classroom (where our recruit school was held), to be formally notified about my promotion and new assignment. On that day all the promotees were dressed in either suits or uniforms and were seated at the desks as the Personnel Division major read out the promotions and new assignments. Being promoted at the same time were several people from my district and watch, one of whom was Ronnie, the former solo bike officer who once tagged me. I sat tensely awaiting my name.

"Dias. District Four Kāneʻohe desk sergeant."

"Sir!" *Yes!* I lived in Kāne'ohe, I had the best three years of my short career in Kāne'ohe, and now I was going to be desk sergeant in Kāne'ohe. *Yes!*

The Personnel Division captain walked up to the major, whispered something to him, and scribbled something on the promotional/transfer list.

"Gary," the major said, "I'm sorry, I made a mistake. A change was made based on seniority and my list wasn't updated. Ronnie?"

"Yes, sir?" he replied.

"Ronnie, you're assigned to District Four Kāne'ohe."

Ronnie's eyes lit up and a big wide grin spread over his face.

"Thank you, sir."

"Gary," said the major, "you're assigned to District One receiving desk."

"Sir," I said aloud. *Shit,* I thought.

I'm absolutely sure that Ronnie's big, wide grin said, *That's what you get for running away from me.*

• • • • •

For the second time in less than five years, I was assigned to the receiving desk. Initially I felt both elated and depressed. I was happy to be promoted. I was now a sergeant. I held rank. The sad part about it was, when we got promoted we lost our motor allowances. It was a difficult time financially for those of us who got promoted to a desk job. We still owned our cars. We still had loan payments to make. We still had auto insurance to maintain. But no motor allowance. Still, we had been promoted. So we hoped that our stay on the desk was going to be a short one.

Mine lasted thirty months. And those thirty months passed very slowly.

17
Wheels Again

Captain Warren Ferreira, who would later become deputy chief, called me into his office and said he had good news and bad news.

"What's the good news?"

"You're being motorized and transferred to the Kalihi Substation."

I didn't kiss him. It would not have been appropriate between supervisor and subordinate.

"The bad news is, you're being suspended for two days in regard to the missing money from the evidence transfer."

I could live with that bad news, because I was getting off the receiving desk. But I didn't believe that I had done anything wrong. Still, I accepted the responsibility for the incident. Some weeks before, on the swing shift, an officer from Kāne'ohe transferred some evidence in a rape/robbery case. The evidence included about two hundred dollars. The officer and evidence came into the receiving desk about ten minutes before I was to get off duty. Since I didn't want to leave work for the arriving desk sergeant, I signed for custody of the evidence, but I held it on the sergeant's desk to turn over to my relief. A few minutes later, my relief came to work, I told him about the evidence, he acknowledged it, and I went home.

At 0700 the next day, I got a call from Captain Thomas Pickard, a.k.a. Aku Eye. He was called Aku Eye by the troops under him because when he scrutinized us, one eye squinted and the other got larger. Tom Pickard was, however, widely known as a fair man. He was from the old school, where common sense ruled, and when an officer chose not to use his common sense, he got that aku eye looking down at him. Tom Pickard was a tall and imposing man. He was also Hawaiian. It's easy to picture him in an earlier era as an ali'i.

The Kalihi Substation. The building housed HPD on the left and the fire department on the right.

He informed me that morning that the bag of evidence was found opened, the money missing, and that mine was the last signature showing custody. I explained to him that I passed it on to the relieving sergeant, but I could feel his piercing eye through the phone line.

"Yours was the last signature. It's your responsibility."

And he was absolutely correct. When we accept a position of authority and rank, we also accept the attendant responsibility and accountability that goes with the position. We eventually learned that another officer stole the money. But the evidence had been my responsibility, and I was accountable for it even though I didn't steal it and wasn't present when it was stolen. The incident taught me a lesson that I took with me through my entire career: as a supervisor I am responsible and accountable for the actions of those I supervise, whether they work on the receiving desk or on the Homicide Detail or are investigating a traffic fatality.

So two days off and two days without pay later, I was a newly motorized sergeant assigned to the Kalihi Substation. My Cutlass

Supreme never really recovered from the high-speed chase that crumpled its front end. So I had to go out and buy a brand new Cordoba. Actor and car spokesman Ricardo Montalban was entirely responsible for my buying that car, with its fine Corinthian leather. It was a coupe, blue with a half-vinyl roof. Bucket seats, air, AM-FM stereo with cassette tape, and a big V-8 engine under the hood. As I drove down Kamehameha IV Road toward the substation, I was feeling pretty sharp. I had a new uniform with new stripes and a new car, the kind sergeants drive. I pulled into the substation's driveway and entered the rear parking lot. There were three other Cordobas in the parking lot just like mine. Popped my bubble. At least the uniform was new. One of the identical Cordobas belonged to another sergeant, Frank Sardinha, who would become my friend and mentor. We responded once to a shooting case. I was on Nimitz Highway and he was on Sand Island Road. We nearly collided in the intersection, and joked later that the investigators would have a hard time figuring out which body and car parts belonged to whom.

The collective personality of the officers of the Kalihi Substation was different from what I was used to. As a group, they thought they were the neglected children of District One. I quickly came to agree with them. Getting information was slow. Getting equipment was slow. Getting replacement officers for vacancies was slow. And because of that, things were run differently.

It was while working in Kalihi that I learned from observing the other sergeants with their officers that the officers are our most precious commodity. The officers in Kalihi were adults who knew their jobs and were allowed to do them. I learned something I would teach to college students twenty years later: Hershey-Blanchard's theory of Situational Leadership. Simply put, a supervisor should *tell* a new employee what and how to do a task; he should direct and support a more experienced officer; and he should delegate a task completely to a very experienced officer. Back then, I didn't know it was a leadership theory; I just knew that it worked. One of the sergeants who followed this theory extraordinarily well was Clifford Kaneaiakala.

Among sergeants, Cliff was widely respected—so much so, that after his retirement he was hired by the police union as a representative.

You could say that this assignment was my initiation to being a field supervisor. I learned how to work with every kind of officer in nearly every situation. There was one situation, however, that no sergeant could have successfully supervised. An officer—we'll call him J. D. (for John Doe)—worked out of Kalihi and drove a departmental blue-and-white car. J. D. was extremely intelligent. In fact, some claimed he held a Ph.D.—in what field, I don't know. I don't even know if he really had a degree at all. But I can tell you this, it wasn't in common sense.

One day at 1445 hours, right after lineup, some of the officers went to the back parking lot to get their cars and then hit the road. A few minutes later, an officer shouted into the station, "If you're parked in a stall along the building, you better move your car right now."

We ran out and saw a blue-and-white facing the row of cars parked next to the building. In front of the blue-and-white was J. D., leaning on the front of the car with his hands on the hood and his feet spread far apart behind him. He had a look of agony on his face. Every third second or so, the blue-and-white lurched six inches closer to the cars parked next to the station house. You see, J. D. started the motor, set the parking brake, put the car in drive for some reason, got out of the car then slammed the driver's door, locking the keys in the car with its motor running. Realizing that the car was lurching forward toward the parked cars, J. D. got in front of it and tried to stop it. Many of the people watching were screaming with laughter. They had already moved any cars that were in the path of the errant car. One of the sergeants told J. D. to get away from the car while another tried to open the locked door with a slim-jim. In a few minutes the front tires of the car were resting against the curb next to the building. Eventually, an officer got the door unlocked, turned the engine off, and gave the keys to J. D. No one got hurt and no property was damaged. A sergeant told J. D. that since he was still at the station, he might as well transport the day shift's paperwork to District One main headquarters. J. D. said okay, but he needed to go to the bathroom first. Understandably.

A long time later, a banging sound came from the locker room in the basement. We went to look. J. D. was standing at his locker in his uniform shirt and underwear, banging on the locker door.

"What the hell you doing?" one of us said.

It seems that J. D. took off his pants and hung them in his locker before he went to the bathroom. Unfortunately, when he shut and locked his locker door, he also locked inside his blue-and-white car keys and his own personal key ring, which contained his locker key, sitting snugly in his pants pocket. We called upstairs and asked the clerk to bring down the spare key to J. D.'s locker. Oops. There was no spare. We had to send an officer to Central Supply Room at District One headquarters to obtain a master key. About an hour later, we got his locker open and J. D. got his pants. By that time, however, an officer had made an arrest and the prisoner needed transport to District One receiving desk. So J. D. was assigned that task. He picked up the prisoner and drove to the receiving desk. There, he escorted the prisoner to the holding cell while the arresting officer briefed the captain, who, that night, was Tom Pickard. Captain Pickard saw J. D. walking around the receiving desk and poked his head out of his office.

"Take your gun off when you come into the receiving desk," called Pickard.

When officers come into the receiving desk, they are required to lock their weapons in a gun box to prevent prisoners from getting hold of an officer's weapon. It seems J. D. was walking around with his gun in his holster, in violation of that policy.

About two hours later, Captain Pickard called the substation and spoke to the clerk. The clerk told me Pickard wanted J. D.'s sergeant to report to him immediately. J. D.'s sergeant went home early that night, so I was it. When I walked into Pickard's office, his aku eye was in full force. On the desk in front of him was a revolver.

"A prisoner found this on the counter and gave it to the desk sergeant. We checked the serial number. It belongs to your J. D."

I wanted to tell Aku Eye that he wasn't *my* J. D., but being technical at that moment might have ended my career. It seems that when Pickard told J. D. to take off his gun when he came into the receiving desk, J. D. took the command literally, unholstered his weapon, placed it on the counter, and went about his business delivering the paperwork he brought with him. I called dispatch and had them notify J. D. to make an immediate 10-1 to Pickard's office. Pickard had me sit on a chair in his office while we waited for J. D. My instructions were clear. J. D. risked everyone's life by leaving in plain sight a loaded revolver, which was found and handled by a prisoner. Suspend him and send him home. Write the report tonight and have it on Pickard's desk before he left for the night.

J. D. arrived and walked into the captain's office.

"Where's your gun?" Aku Eye managed to say, looking with disbelief at the patrol officer standing in front of him with an empty holster.

"In my holster, sir." J. D. didn't even bother to look down.

The aku eye got really big and stared at me. I grabbed J. D. by the arm and took him outside, where I told him what had happened. His response to me was classic.

"Boy, you make one mistake and they stomp all over you."

18
Image Is Everything

Command presence. I never heard of the term until I began taking courses toward my master's degree. Yet every police officer knows exactly what it means. More than knowing what it means, we all know it as a way of *being*. It is who we are when we put that uniform on. Command presence is a spirit, an essence—an *image* of who we are as police officers. Officers must portray strength, knowledge, determination, and control at all times.

Command presence most nearly equals self-confidence. It does not mean that civility or politeness goes out the window. The opposite is true. Civility and politeness along with a firm voice and an image of knowledge and control are much more effective than a position of either meekness or aggression. In some situations, in fact, meekness can be fatal.

"Ah, sir . . . could you . . . I mean . . . would you please consider getting out of your car? . . . Of course, please take your time . . . I'm *so* sorry for inconveniencing you," is not what to say when demanding a criminal get out of his car in order to be arrested.

One night I watched a young recruit trying to persuade a driver to get out of his car. We were at the police academy in Waipahu. I had just finished conducting a class on crime-scene investigation and was speaking to the sergeant of another recruit class. His class was role-playing mock crime scenes, and one recruit was dealing with a stubborn driver who had a warrant of arrest for robbery. I watched and listened as the young, inexperienced officer cajoled, prodded, and even begged the driver to come out of the car so he could effect an arrest. The driver (a civilian volunteer) simply sat in the car, door closed, window down, and refused to budge or even acknowledge the officer, according to his instructions from the sergeant.

As the sergeant and I spoke, minutes ticked by and the recruit sank deeper and deeper into a situation he would not be able to get out of. My blood pressure slowly rose. My patience dwindled. Didn't this recruit realize he was placing himself and any other officer in the area in danger? What if this man wanted for robbery had a weapon? What if he decided to flee? Jesus, recruit! Think of the consequences of your inaction. I couldn't take it anymore, and I abandoned my conversation with the sergeant and approached the recruit.

"That's not how to get this guy out of his car," I said to him, sounding pretty disgusted. "This is how it's done."

"Get out of the frickin' car!" I demanded of the driver as I yanked open the driver's door. I grabbed the actor by his elbow, pulled him out of the seat, put him up against the side of the car, and cuffed him. It took all of five seconds.

The recruit stood there blinking. His sergeant came up. He was very polite.

"Ah, Lieutenant, thank you for your assistance, but, ah, we have this under control now."

I slunk away, embarrassed. My response didn't fit the role of instructor that night, and in the future I left the handling of insecure recruits to their sergeants.

But speaking of roles, a police officer's roles are widely varied. Cop, counselor, teacher, giver of first aid, not to mention son, daughter, father, wife, family provider, friend, and neighbor are some of the roles a police officer may play every day. We relate to people through our roles. Some officers see themselves entirely in the context of one role. Sometimes officers are more successful as police officers than as husbands, for example. Others are more successful taking on multiple roles and responding to various needs.

In their roles, police officers look at themselves in different ways. To some, being a police officer is not much different from performing any other civilian job. It's work. To others, it's a lifestyle. And depending on who that officer is, that lifestyle can get pretty outrageous. I've seen guys develop **Deep Low VOICES** and end up sounding like Barry White of the disco generation or James Earl Jones, a.k.a. Darth Vader, because that's how they believe a police officer should sound. It's so funny to hear a guy who sounds normal during lineup become a super bass when he hits the road. In addition to the deep voices, certain other bodily changes occur. The unbending metal rod appears in the spine of a few, from the top of the head to the tailbone. A few metamorphose into Sylvester Stallone, including the look and the walk, as if they were suffering from a rash.

And a few watch too much TV. One detective always wore clothing from thirties and forties private eye movies: the baggy pants, the white dress shirt with sleeves rolled up, the necktie loose around an unbuttoned collar. To round off the look, he carried a snub-nosed revolver in a shoulder holster hanging in his armpit and a bottomless cup of coffee, and had the neverending cigarette glued to his lower lip. If he could have gotten away with a fedora, I'm sure he would have.

And there were those who just didn't care what they looked like. I ran into an officer recently whose belly hung over his belt and covered his buckle. His pants hung so low on his hips I actually expected to see his buttocks when he turned. His gun hung so low down his leg, he would have to lean over to draw his weapon. His uniform was dirty and wrinkled and smelled of too many days of use. His slovenly image told a very different story from the one HPD wants to portray. He was a sad sight, and I hoped as I left that one of his supervisors would impress upon him the need to change that look.

Image is everything. People get their images of the police from the officers they have contact with. They get their opinions from interacting with officers, from speaking with friends and relatives who have interacted with officers, and from news stories about the police. Members of the public who are victims of crime or subjects of traffic control or who are simply lost and asking directions also interact with the police and form opinions of them. In each case, the behavior of the officer shapes that citizen's opinion.

When I was the commander of the Traffic Division, the Solo Bike Detail came under my command. These officers looked crisp and sharp: uniforms always clean and pressed; tall leather boots, belt, holster, and accessories always shiny; helmets brilliant white. All the officers were physically fit. And each one wore dark glasses. I couldn't understand why so many complaints came in that the officers were rude and overbearing. I knew them all, and they were not rude and overbearing in everyday life. I was puzzled until I watched one of them issue a citation one day.

He pulled the speeding car over, slowly walked up to the driver, explained what the citation was for, obtained the driver's license, and issued the citation. No rudeness. No overbearing conduct. But from even my neutral standpoint, he looked like a storm trooper. The most imposing aspect was that you couldn't see much of his face. Between the helmet and his dark glasses, you could see only part of his nose, lips, and jaw. And it dawned on me: in our society, we look into each other's eyes when we speak. It's one of the ways we sense the person to whom we're speaking. The dark glasses and helmet that covered the officer's eyes and head eliminated this means of sensing that, even though he was issuing a tag, he was human. I tried to get the officers to remove their helmets and glasses when issuing tags. No way! It was part of the image the officers had of themselves. It was part of being a solo bike officer. I gave in and didn't push the issue. The storm trooper image prevailed.

A traffic citation is the most common encounter a citizen has with the police. And it's a negative one. The citizen may have to go to court, pay a fine. His insurance may go up. It's a bad experience all around. One of my early supervisors once said that if we could get traffic violators to say, "Thank you, officer," as they left, we were successful in issuing the tag and expressing a positive image of ourselves and the department. (Actually, you'd be surprised how many people really do say "thank you" after getting tagged.)

A big shaper of public opinion and the image of officers and departments is response time to calls for help. It has been traditionally assumed that the faster the response time to a crime scene, the better chance the officer has of apprehending criminals. Studies have shown, however, that response time is perceived differently by police officers and citizens.

Response-time perception is closely associated with preventive patrol—the random movement through the community by officers on the lookout for crime. One of the most important studies on preventive patrol was conducted in 1972 with the Kansas City Police Department. The study was designed to answer the question, "Do police officers on random patrol actually prevent crime?" The study used three types of beats. The *reactive beats* had no officers assigned to them, no preventive patrol. Officers were allowed to enter and handle, or pass through in response to cases, but could not patrol in the reactive beats. The *control beats* had the normal complement of officers—one officer per beat. The *proactive beats* increased police visibility and patrols two to three times above their usual level.

The hypothesis was that if preventive patrol actually deterred crime, there would be substantially less crime in the proactive beats.

After one year of analysis, the results showed no significant differences in the level of crime in any of the beats. It also showed no significant changes in the perception of citizens in regard to police presence in their neighborhoods, and no significant changes in the perception of citizens' satisfaction with response times.

The main determinant of citizen satisfaction is a citizen's perception of the police and expectation of the response time. For example, if you come home and find your child's tricycle missing from your garage, you call the police and ask for an officer to come handle your complaint. The officer arrives fifteen minutes after you call. For the average person, this response time is acceptable. You call the police, go about your business, the police arrive, and you file your complaint about the missing trike. However, if a burglar armed with a knife attacks your spouse, you will call the police and expect them to arrive quickly. If an officer is just around the corner, gets there in seconds, and saves your spouse, you think the officer is godlike and can do no wrong. But if an officer isn't close by and arrives three minutes after your call (the national average), those three minutes may feel like three hours and you now question what took him or her so long, especially if your spouse was injured.

The amount of response time is not the issue. What matters most is whether the response time meets the citizen's expectation for the response. If the response takes longer than callers expect, they will be less satisfied.

Using this knowledge, departments took advantage of citizens' expectations and developed a concept called *differential police response*. Traditionally, police were dispatched to cases in the order that requests for help were received, except for life-threatening emergencies. This new strategy recognizes that the response to a noncritical call—the theft of a tricycle, for example—can be completed over the telephone. What is important to citizens is that they receive immediate responses to their calls for service, regardless of how minor they may seem.

An example of the importance of officer behavior and image occurred early one morning when, as a member of the Homicide Detail, I responded to a murder at a bar in Waipahu. Two men had argued, gone outside, and become involved in a fistfight. The loser of the fight went to his truck, got a gun, and shot and killed the other man. Then he jumped into the truck and took off. Officers arrived and secured the scene, called for the Homicide Detail, and canvassed the area for witnesses. We arrived and began our investigation. One detective was assigned to the crime scene investigation, the other to speak to witnesses.

One enthusiastic officer went across Farrington Highway and found a man who would turn out to be a key witness. The man, who had been sitting in his car drinking a cup of coffee and eating a donut, witnessed the confrontation and killing. Thinking it would be important, he wrote down the license plate number of the suspect's truck on the only surface he had at the time—the palm of his hand. He watched the police and then the detectives arrive. The officer found him, took him to the scene, and approached one of the detectives. The detective's response was devastating.

"Can't you see I'm busy? Tell him to go sit down. I'll get to him when I can," was the abrasive response from the detective. I couldn't believe one of my detectives would speak so crudely to a witness to a murder.

The witness's response was what I expected and feared.

"F—k you guys."

He walked back across the street, got in his car, and left. The officer who found him had written down his name and pertinent information, including the license number of the killer's truck, but here was an eyewitness to the murder whom we just ticked off. I sent an officer after him to apologize and bring him back. The witness refused to accept the apology. We eventually spoke to him at his residence, apologizing profusely for the inconsiderate actions of that detective, but with no luck. The man was so offended that his response to us now was that he didn't remember anything. Fortunately, with the license plate number he initially provided, we were able to identify the killer and charge him with murder. The detective voluntarily left the Homicide Detail shortly after that investigation.

The perception that witness had of us was poor. We were rude to him, and he was not going to forget it. And I'll bet he told everyone he knew how badly that detective behaved.

Image is everything.

• • • • •

So if you're driving down the Pali Highway one day and you're pulled over and tagged by a solo bike officer complete with helmet and shades, just smile and say thank you. Toss in that he has great eyes. He'll be in a state of confusion the rest of the shift.

19
Sector Seven

Working in the Kalihi area as a swing sergeant was a good assignment, but it wasn't as satisfying as having my own sector would have been. As a swing sergeant, I was responsible for a sector for that shift only. I didn't have many other responsibilities in regard to sector operations. Each day, my duties consisted of responding to any serious cases that might occur in the sector I was assigned to or assisting with any immediate needs of the officers in that sector. Then one day I learned that several sergeants from my watch were going to be promoted to lieutenant. I submitted my request to be considered for a permanent sector—and lit a few candles.

My prayers were answered, and I was assigned as the permanent Sector Seven sergeant for Bravo Watch. It turned out to be one of my favorite assignments. Sector Seven was in a part of Honolulu that was busy, but not busy enough to cause an officer to feel like a stenographer moving from one case to another, and not slow enough to be boring. The sector extended from Punchbowl Street to Pi'ikoi Street and from the H-1 to the ocean. Some of its major landmarks included The Queen's Medical Center, Honolulu Hale (City Hall), the Kaka'ako business area, Kewalo Basin, and Ala Moana Beach Park. The beat numbers when I was Seven's sergeant were 46, 47, 51, 54, 57, and 59, and my new call number was 169.

We had a little bit of everything in Sector Seven: the city government headquarters, strips of private businesses along King and Beretania streets and Kapi'olani Boulevard, a light industrial area, residential neighborhoods, a number of bars, two hospitals, and the biggest park on O'ahu. A good variety of incidents occurred simply as a result of the varied mixture of land zoning in our area. Unlike officers in sectors confined to residential areas, Seven's officers were treated to every kind of criminal investigation on the books.

One of those treats was getting to go to the mayor's office. On one such day I was the only available officer, so I was sent to Mayor Frank Fasi's office on a complaint of a male creating a disturbance. Upon my arrival the mayor and his staff were talking with a man who kept repeating that the mayor was not listening to the will of the people. Mayor Fasi smiled at me and explained over the objections of the irate visitor that he had exhausted all discussion and means to satisfy the man and now wanted the man to leave.

Even before I spoke, the man said, "Okay, Officer, no pilikia. I'm leaving. But I want to ask you, when I have a complaint to make against you, I call the chief of police. Who do I call when I have a complaint against Mayor Fasi?"

"I don't know," I answered. "The governor?"

Well, I learned double quick that the mayor didn't appreciate my answer. He shot me a dirty look and frostily informed me that he didn't answer to the governor. Hizzoner wasn't smiling when I left his executive suite. Oh, well.

Perhaps the best aspect of the sector was its personnel. As varied as Seven was, so were my patrol officers. I felt blessed to have the group I had. Bill, our Beat 46 officer, was the sector's "old man," in his mid-thirties. From Missouri, Bill held a master's degree in Russian Studies and was recently out of the navy. Mitch had a teaching degree and did a little teaching before the lure of HPD pulled him away from the public schools. Mitch usually relieved 51 and 54. Mike, our 47 officer, was just a little younger than Bill and was the primary instigator of all the pranks we pulled on each other. Ricky, who covered 54, was a bit more serious than the rest, and Norman, our 59 man, was—well, Norman was Norman. Coming from District Four, I was more than willing to participate in the sector's jokes and pranks, and there were a few really good ones.

A relief officer worked in the sector every now and then, when one of our regulars was on extended time off. This relief officer was an okay guy, but didn't like the pranks that got pulled occasionally. I don't want to give the impression that all we did was play jokes on each other. Far from it. Seven's officers were among the hardest-working groups in town. But when we had a little slow time, or if an opportunity arose, we grabbed the opportunity. So one day the relief guy parked his blue-and-white in the McDonald's parking lot and went for a ride with Bill, who was breaking him in to Beat 46. Unfortunately for the relief guy, he parked next to a dumpster full of palm fronds recently trimmed from nearby trees. No one ever admitted to burying his car under a mountain of palm fronds.

None of us, though, had the creativity that Mike had when it came to playing pranks. One night he placed a traffic cone over the blue light of our lieutenant's car. The man drove most of the night with what looked like a glowing orange dunce cap coming from the top of his car.

Another time, Mike searched the junkyards until he found an old gas station pump. He cut off the nozzle with about a foot of hose remaining and frayed the end of it. Then he waited for Norman to put gas in his car one day. Later that night, he placed the nozzle into his gas tank.

"My God, Norman did you fill gas today?"

"Yeah, why?"

"You drove off without taking the nozzle out of your tank."

Norman looked out his car window and saw the nozzle and frayed rubber hose sticking out of his gas tank.

"Oh, Jesus!" said Norman. He started up his car and drove back to the police gas pumps to face the music. The old dispenser wobbled in the wind as he drove off down Young Street.

I wasn't immune from Mike's pranks either. Every year, each division undergoes an inspection conducted by the Internal Affairs unit. The department's facility is inspected, as well as its personnel and their cars. The car checks were detailed. Everything was looked at, from the condition of the car to its odometer. Mike took great pains one year to craft a replacement license plate for me. He swapped mine for the new one he made a day or so before it was my turn to have my car inspected. Unbeknownst to me, the entire sector was watching from across the street as I drove up to the radio shop to meet with the Internal Affairs inspector. Everything went fairly well until the inspector asked me to open my trunk.

"How long have you had that license plate?" he asked, in a normal tone of voice.

"Since I bought the car," I answered, without even bothering to look.

"Did the chief approve the special plates?"

I looked puzzled, and he pointed to my license plate. Instead of my authorized plate, there was an exact replica of a plate inside my license plate holder. "BOZO" it read.

I must have stood there for too long a time with my jaw hanging, staring at my BOZO special plate. The detective tapped my shoulder and raised his eyebrows in a questioning look as I turned toward him.

"Ha, ha," I tried to laugh. "Someone is playing a joke on me."

"Ha, ha. How about you come back tomorrow with your normal plates."

"Okay." I got in my car and drove off while keying my microphone.

"One-six-nine to four-seven. What's your ten-five?"

Yes, we played jokes on one another, but we also were determined to be the best we could be, to paraphrase the army's slogan.

One night we received notification of an alarm going off at a Pay 'n Save Store on Ala Moana Boulevard across from Kewalo Basin, where The Ward Centre is today. Bill was the first to arrive, and he reported that a window had been smashed. Several of us arrived a minute or so later. Bill's car was there. We entered the store through the broken window and began a search of the store. No Bill. I was becoming concerned. At that time, the department had only enough portable radios for each sergeant to have one. I had no means of calling for Bill if he was on foot away from his car. We completed the search of the entire store and met up with the alarm company representative, who arrived after us, and, later, the store manager who came down to secure the premises. Still no Bill.

Then the dispatcher called me.

"Central to one-six-nine."

"One-six-nine, by"

"We have a report of a police officer sitting on the curb on Punchbowl Street at The Queen's Medical Center. Do you have someone who can check on this?"

"Ten-four. I'm proceeding."

I got to Punchbowl and Beretania in a few minutes, and there was Bill, sitting on the curb, with his feet in the street, leaning forward with his elbows on his knees. Lying on the sidewalk next to him was a man, his hands cuffed behind his back. I parked and got out of my car.

" 'Bout time someone came to pick me up."

We learned that when Bill parked his car on Ala Moana Boulevard and was walking to the broken window, the man he now had in cuffs jumped out of the store and began running. Bill gave chase. And chased and chased. He said that the closest he got to the suspect was about ten feet, and every time the suspect looked behind to see if the cop was still chasing him, he was able to put on a short burst of speed. Bill said the crook never tried to cut through buildings, but stayed on the sidewalk during the entire pursuit. He added that by the time they neared Queen's, both he and the suspect could manage only a slow jog. It was the suspect who finally spoke.

"What? You not goin' give up?"

"Nope."

"Okay, I quit. You win."

Bill said he handcuffed the man and they both sat down on the curb, trying to catch their breaths. The suspect told him, "I goin' sleep," and lay back on the sidewalk. He was tempted to join him, Bill said, but figured it would present a poor image.

We joked for a long time that the sector's "old man" still had it in him, leaping buildings in a single bound and running from Ala

Moana to The Queen's Medical Center without passing out or having a heart attack.

Bill actually did have a mild heart attack about a year later. Queen's was on Bill's beat, and he spent many a long hour there doing hospital follow-ups for the rest of the island. He got to know the nurses and doctors pretty well. When he suffered his heart attack, he drove himself to Queen's and we met him there. Twenty-one years after this incident, I can still remember the evil smile on the face of the emergency room nurse who came to his bedside.

"We're going to have to put in a catheter."

"In where?" Bill asked suspiciously.

"We don't want you getting up to go to the bathroom, so we're going to insert a catheter."

"Bring it on," he said, with a look of determination. My knees were getting weak, so I excused myself and went into the hall.

Bill's wife, Jane, arrived a few minutes later in a taxi. We soon learned that Bill was doing fine but was going to be kept overnight for observation. I called my lieutenant and told him I would be back on the road as soon as I took Bill's wife home. The lieutenant didn't want me to do that. He said I should return to the field and she could take a cab home. It was one of the occasional times during my career that I heard utter nonsense come from the mouth of a police official. I shrugged. It had been about a year since I got suspended and I was due. I politely told the lieutenant I was taking Bill's wife home. He was one of my officers, and I was going to take care of him and his family. Then I hung up. It felt good.

I took Jane home and offered any assistance she may have needed. Then I returned to the sector. It was perhaps the first time I felt overt satisfaction at helping take care of someone who worked for me. It felt good to help Bill. It felt good to help a family member of someone on my staff. It felt as if we were family, that we were much more than supervisor and subordinate. We were part of Sector Seven, and we took care of each other.

When I returned to the station later that night after our tour of

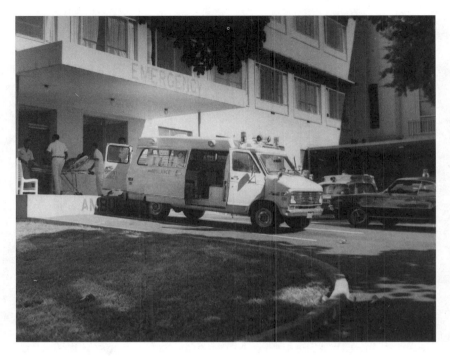

The Queen's Medical Center emergency room entrance in the mid-seventies

duty, I expected the lieutenant to call me into his office and discipline me for refusing to follow his instructions. He never said anything to me that night. In fact, he never mentioned it. Perhaps his good sense returned from whatever break it was on.

I had one telephone call to make before I left for the night.

"Hey, Bill. Did I wake you?"

"No, I was watching Johnny Carson. What's up?"

"We decided to help you out. I'm bringing the sector down and we'll yank out that catheter."

Click.

20
Simply Norman

Imagine a bull with a crew cut that falls to one side. He's kind of stocky. Not fat. Stocky. The bull does everything bulls are supposed to do, and does it well. He's a little stubborn. Sometimes, when he's got his mind set on something, he's a whole lot of stubborn. The bull likes things to be simple. He avoids complicated situations. He's a little myopic, but he'll do whatever it is he's instructed to do. He's dependable, he's courageous, and he's likable.

That's Norman.

Norman worked the Kaka'ako and Ala Moana end of Sector Seven. Sometimes the things Norman did seemed just a bit eccentric. He came to Hawai'i after his tour of duty in Vietnam, and that may have had something to do with his eccentricity. Some people described Norman as being more simple than eccentric. I think he was a bit of both, but he also had a great sense of humor and great timing. He wasn't always pulling pranks, like Mike, but he was very quick on the uptake if a situation presented itself.

"One-six-nine to five-seven."

"Standing by, Sarge."

"What's your ten-five for a ten-three?"

"Queen and Punchbowl."

"Ten-four."

I proceeded toward the intersection of Queen and Punchbowl streets to meet with Norman. A few seconds after his transmission, and before I traveled very far at all, came another transmission.

"Queen and South."

A few seconds later . . .

"Queen and Coral."

And then . . .

"Queen and Cooke."

I realized he was traveling in the Diamond Head direction on Queen Street and was calling out the intersecting streets as he passed them. Was he kidding, or was he simply being Norman?

"Norman!"

"Standing by, Sarge."

"Park your car and tell me where you're parked."

"Queen and Ward."

Norman's tour of duty in Vietnam made him very conscious of rank. He believed that his sergeant absolutely should not, and if he was around would not be the first officer to enter a dark warehouse in response to a burglary alarm, for example. We responded to such an alarm at a Kaka'ako building one night. I pulled into the parking lot just ahead of Norman, and my headlights illuminated an open door. I got out of my car, looked at Norman, and pointed to the door. Norman nodded that he understood. I got to the door and was just about to step inside when I was suddenly grabbed by the back of my collar and pulled violently backward. Norman stepped in front, whispering, "Sergeants don't go in first."

We searched the warehouse, and Norman found a young man hiding behind some boxes. He was probably in his late teens. After searching and cuffing him, Norman was surprisingly gentle with the young burglar. In no time, the kid admitted that he and his friend broke in to see what they could steal, but found nothing worthwhile. Just as they were leaving, we pulled up. His friend managed to escape into the dark, but he was afraid and went back inside to hide. I was impressed with Norman's handling of the incident. He could have simply cuffed the kid and taken him in, but he took the time to try to create a bond, no matter how thin, and turn him away from crime. He encouraged him to come back after he dealt with this burglary issue and meet with him to work out problems. I was touched by his gentleness and humanity in a situation that could have been routine. I realized that this, also, was simply Norman.

I spoke with him later about yanking me by the collar. He said it was his job to be the line officer. It was his responsibility to enter the warehouse first. It was his risk.

"Sergeants don't go first."

I sensed that there was something deeper than what he had described, but I also felt the time wasn't right to probe. Some time later, when I was alone with him, I remembered the warehouse incident and commended him again for his handling of the kid. He mentioned that he met with him once after the incident and bought him lunch. The kid seemed sincere, but he hadn't seen him since. I used the opportunity to explore my suspicions that there was more to his needing to go first into that warehouse, and I asked him why I couldn't enter a scene first. He had a one-sentence answer and I didn't push it any further.

"I lost my sergeant in Vietnam, and it should have been me."

• • • • •

Norman was a last-minute guy when it came to lineups. He would rush in just before one of us called the troops to attention. One afternoon we were going to be inspected by newly promoted Major Pickard, a.k.a. Aku Eye. When I checked, everyone in my sector was present, except Norman. I looked at my watch; he had about two minutes. All of a sudden, Norman rushed into the squad room and swept past the others, who were beginning to line up in three ranks. The sergeants gathered at one end in a rank of their own.

The sergeant who was squad leader that day stood in front of the ranks, and Major Pickard stood behind him, smiling at the men preparing to hit the streets. Major Pickard seemed to be in a good mood. The squad leader gave a few instructions to several of the officers, and I knew he was stalling, giving Norman just a few seconds more to make the inspection.

The swinging door to the locker room flew open with a bang, and Norman ran to the end of the middle rank. As soon as he was in place,

Chief Francis Keala issuing a commendation during lineup in the seventies

the squad leader called the troops to attention.

" 'Ten-hut!"

Everyone snapped to attention.

"Dress right. . . . Dress! . . . Ready, front! . . . First rank, remain at attention! . . . Second and third ranks, parade rest!"

Major Pickard began his inspection of the first rank. He moved from officer to officer, inspecting each man from hat to shoes. He was still smiling, and occasionally he made small talk with the officer he was inspecting. Everyone was breathing a little easier. It seemed the inspection was going well.

"First rank, parade rest! . . . Second rank, 'ten-hut!"

Major Pickard began his inspection of the second rank. He was still smiling. It was a good day. Pickard got to the end of the line, where Norman was standing straight as a two-by-four. Pickard's smile seemed to wane a little as he inspected Norman. I began to pay more attention.

I need to tell you here that Norman had a foot problem. I'm not sure exactly what it was. It could have been athlete's foot, or it could have been something else—I just don't know. I do know that every day, Norman dusted a white powder on his feet before he put on his socks. On this particular day, when he dusted his feet, he got white powder on his bright, shiny shoes.

Major Pickard looked him up and down, and when he got to his shoes, noticed the white powder.

"You have white powder on your shoes," everyone heard Major Pickard tell Norman.

Norman looked down at his shoes and without speaking did the only thing that seemed right at the time. He wiped the top of each shoe on the back of the opposite pant leg. Pickard's smile disappeared, and his mouth hung open ever so slightly. I was squinting and leaning forward to get a better look.

Pickard leaned around Norman to look at the back of his pants.

"Now you have white powder on the back of your pants."

A few ripples of soft laughter came from the third rank.

Norman twisted a little and looked at the back of his pants. That wouldn't do. After all, this was an inspection. Turning a little away from the major, he bent over and dusted off his pant legs with his hands. Then he faced the front and came again to attention. A few more ripples of laughter. I was in a full sweat.

Pickard stood in front of Norman. His mouth was still slightly open, in disbelief, as he looked down at Norman's hands. Norman's eyes followed Pickard's gaze. He suddenly realized that his hands were covered in white powder and instinctively wiped his hands down the front of his uniform shirt.

The shift erupted into screams of laughter. Norman stood ramrod straight, and the big aku eye stared down the aisle at me.

"Come see me," Pickard said to me as he walked from the ranks and left the squad room on his way back to his office.

No one could be angry at Norman for long. He always meant well, and he always tried so very hard.

Years later, I worked as a lieutenant in the Criminal Investigation Division. One day another detective came up to me and asked, "Did you hear? Somebody shot Norman."

Every day that Norman worked for me, he wore a bulletproof vest. The day he was shot was hot. It was his last day of work before he was to take his scheduled vacation. There were only a few more minutes of work left in the day, and Norman took off his vest. Shortly before the end of the shift, Norman pulled over a traffic violator. He walked up to the driver's window, as he had done hundreds of times before. This time, the driver leaned out of the window and shot Norman in the stomach with a .45-caliber handgun.

Norman managed to get back to his car and call for help. The suspect fled. Norman was taken to The Queen's Medical Center, where he remained in critical condition for several days. Because he was shot in the stomach, it took a long time for him to recover. He never did return to Sector Seven. Instead he retired and returned to his home on the mainland.

The guy who shot Norman was eventually caught and convicted of attempted murder in the first degree and sentenced to life in prison.

21
Women in Law Enforcement

Law enforcement was a male sport until the mid-seventies, when women began infiltrating departments across the United States. No, I'm not prejudiced against women in law enforcement, but that was the prevailing attitude across the mainland and in Hawai'i when members of the "weaker" sex wanted to become police officers. Some of the male officers cited every excuse in the book as to why women should not become police officers. In fact, they wrote that book. It was a work of fiction.

Here are a few of those myths:
- Women are not as strong as men and cannot pull their own weight in a fight.
- Male officers will have to spend their time watching after the female officers to keep them from getting into trouble.
- Male suspects will not respect women.
- Women will use their feminine charms to advance in rank within the department.
- Woman cannot deal with the stress associated with police work.
- Women are not as intelligent as men.
- Law enforcement is a male career.

Twenty-five years after women broke through the barriers to a law enforcement career, nationally one officer in eight is a woman. Ten percent of HPD's officers are women. These female officers are generally better educated than their male counterparts. Women recognized that entering a male-dominated profession would be difficult. Consequently, their goals included completing college before applying to a department. Nationally, studies have shown that approximately 30 percent of female officers hold graduate degrees, as compared with only 3 percent of male officers.

In Hawai'i, before the first woman was hired as a police officer, the department hired women to work in the old Juvenile Crime Prevention Division. Their primary job was to work with juvenile offenders. The first women patrol officers weren't hired by HPD until the last half of the seventies.

Perhaps the most accomplished woman police officer in Hawai'i during the last thirty years of the twentieth century was Barbara Uphouse Wong. Barbara started her career as a dispatcher. By the time she retired, she achieved the rank of assistant chief. Barbara is an achiever. After she retired, she had another goal in mind and enrolled in the University of Hawai'i's Richardson School of Law.

One of the first women hired by the department was assigned to Sector Seven. Kaui was in her early twenties when she joined HPD and became one of our blue-and-white car relief officers. Those first few months with Kaui on the beat were difficult for us as well as for her. The officers didn't know how to treat her. Some were overly protective; some were overly cautious. One male officer or another would follow her from case to case—just in case she needed help. Kaui noticed this and soon became frustrated with it. One day the dam burst. We were at McDonald's having a sector meeting (that's the excuse we give when more than three of us gather at the same spot) when she was sent to a domestic argument on Kīna'u Street. As she stood to respond, two other male officers also got up. Kaui blew up. "I can handle this by myself," she said. She jumped into her blue-and-white and left. The other officers argued with me briefly that working in Seven was all about teamwork, and she was overreacting. A few minutes later I relented and we all proceeded to her location.

When we arrived, Kaui was in the process of arresting a man whom she witnessed assaulting a woman. He didn't want to be arrested and was giving her a hard time. When the other officers arrived, the man gave up and allowed Kaui to handcuff him. Kaui was pissed. She thought we didn't give her the chance to make her own arrest. We held a meeting to resolve the problem. Kaui came to understand that police work required teamwork, and the male officers came to realize that Kaui was a capable police officer.

One day, Kaui was sent to the Honolulu Municipal Building parking lot to handle a car break-in. The owner of the car was the city director of parks and recreation. The director was upset that the break-in occurred in the first place, and was adamant that Kaui search diligently for latent fingerprints. He left her to complete her work and returned to his office. Kaui followed his instructions and did a good job dusting his car's interior—the dash, the glove box, the steering wheel, the door panels, everywhere she could in her search for latents.

In dusting for latent fingerprints, the officer applies a black graphite powder to surfaces with either a feather or nylon brush. The powder sticks to the oils and acids placed on a surface by fingers in the form of latent fingerprints. The powder is very fine and leaves a film of black graphite everywhere.

Kaui finished her task, recovered a number of latent fingerprints, and returned to her beat. Later that evening I received a call from dispatch.

"Dispatch to one-six-nine."

"One-six-nine standing by."

"Make an immediate ten-one to the chief's office."

"To the chief's office?"

"Ten-four, number one's office."

I went as quickly as I could. I got to his office, knocked on his door, and was invited in. I walked inside and came to an abrupt halt. There, sitting in front of the chief's desk, were the city director of parks and recreation and his wife. Both of them were dressed in white evening wear, she in a fancy white evening gown, he in a white tux. Both of them were covered from head to foot in grayish black dust. The director's wife had slender streaks of black running from her eyes down her cheeks. On her gown were little black drops where her tears fell onto her lap.

I knew exactly what had happened. The director and his wife got into their car from opposite sides without cleaning the interior. They slammed their doors at the same time and POOF! The air pressure changed, and billions of carbon powder particles burst into the air and filled the interior of the car with a black cloud. The sight of them sitting in the chief's office—a contrast in black and white—was hilarious, and I wanted to laugh, yet I knew laughing at that moment would be disastrous for my continuing employment.

The chief wanted an explanation, and apparently mine was not sufficient. He wanted me to conduct an investigation and report back to him the next day. And to inform him who was going to pay to replace the director and his wife's clothing.

"Yes, sir."

My investigation was simple. Kaui did nothing wrong, and I said so in my report. In fact, she did a good job in her investigation, and I said so to the chief. It was not her obligation to clean up the director's car. In regard to his clothing, I believed he was responsible for the replacement. After all, he knew the police officer was dusting his car, and doing an even more thorough job at his own request. I felt offended that the patrol officer was being held responsible for the director's unthinking rush to enter his car without first checking for carbon powder on his seat.

My report went upstairs, and an inspector ("inspector" was a former rank of HPD's between major and assistant chief), called me to his office. My report was unacceptable. How dare I say Kaui did nothing wrong? The inspector instructed me to resubmit my report and discipline Kaui for the incident. I refused, and in a moment of anger told the inspector I would take this matter to the union. That was the last I heard of it—for about eight months. During the annual performance evaluations, when I pulled Kaui's personnel file for review, I saw that my report to the chief had been altered and my signature forged to show that Kaui had been disciplined.

Imagine that! Someone from the department retyped my report and forged my signature. I wonder who it was? I took the altered report to the Personnel Division and demanded to review the rest of Kaui's file to see if any other copies of the forged report were in her docket. I then went to my commander and told him I was taking the issue to the union. I did. It never went anywhere. I was ashamed that, in order to placate a politician, someone allowed or even encouraged a forgery that could have had a negative effect on an officer's career. The incident also alerted me that supervisors should occasionally check the personnel files of those who serve under them.

22
Kawaiāha'o Church and Mission Houses

When police officers get together and tell ghost stories, the stories are usually about some other officer at some other place during some other decade. But in Sector Seven, we had our own haunted house. Or I should say, church.

Kawaiāha'o Church, its graveyard, its preschool building, and its neighboring mission houses provided us with many a spooky night during my tour of duty in Sector Seven. It all started with the water sprinklers.

We were on the First Watch (graveyard shift—no pun intended) and had received information from the previous shifts that the maintenance staff at Kawaiāha'o were complaining that someone was turning on their water-sprinkler system at night. This had happened several times a week for the past few weeks. It had to be kids pulling this prank. Who else? Our sector got together and discussed how we were going to stake out the church.

"We need to put a car at city hall, in the mayor's parking stall."

"Yeah, right. What about in his office; it overlooks the church."

"Fasi would really like that."

"Okay, you guys, get serious," I said.

Mike took over. "All right, we put Bill in the King Street driveway of city hall. I'll park at the supreme court building. Norman waits on Queen Street. When the kids come, we throw the trap."

It sounded good. That first night . . . nothing. The second night . . . nothing. A week went by . . . nothing happened. We began to let up a little. When you sit in stake-out night after night and nothing happens you begin to think that you were "burned." Or the pranksters simply went away. But the very first night that we did not provide a stake-out, the water sprinklers went on. This series of failed stake-outs, with water sprinklers going on when we weren't there, went on for a month. The sector was getting frustrated. Our major was getting frustrated. We were determined to catch the people responsible because now they were toying with us. Then it happened.

One night as we watched the property, the water sprinklers came on. In literally seconds, we were on the grounds. Mike, Bill, Mitch, and I went in through the Punchbowl entrance. Norman and Ricky came in from Mission Lane. No one. Only the sprinklers running. We missed 'em. The next night, we pulled the trap in a little closer. Everyone moved closer to the driveways. The sprinklers went on again. Again, no more than a few seconds went by before we were on the grounds. Again no one. Okay. We left people on King, Punchbowl, Queen, and Mission Lane, and only two of us went in. We'll catch 'em when they flee the grounds. The sprinklers went on again. No one left the grounds.

One of the maintenance men told us he believed spirits were turning on the water sprinklers. He said that every so often, something unexplainable happened on the church grounds, and he thought this was one of those times. "Nah," said Mike, a disbeliever. It had to be someone. But the man was persistent, so the next night we waited on the grounds with the maintenance building in front of us and the controls of the water sprinkler system in full sight. With us was the maintenance man who believed that Hawaiian spirits were responsible for turning on the water. He was not happy to be there. Not one of us, however, expected anything to happen, and it was a slow night, so we just parked and talked. Someone went for coffee and food and we sat and watched and waited.

Then the sprinklers went on. They started slowly, just as they would if someone turned the valve open in a normal fashion, and increased to full pressure. We ran up to the maintenance building with the maintenance man behind us. No one was there.

"Any other valves?" someone yelled, as we circled the building.

"No, just this one," the man shouted back.

"There's a malfunction in the system," someone said.

"How the hell could there be a malfunction in a valve? The damn thing has to be turned in order for the water to flow."

"I was watching. There was no one at the valve. And the water came on."

Mitch was very quiet, and I asked him what he thought.

"I don't like this. I don't like this at all."

Someone got a call, and it was time to get back to our beats. The maintenance man looked sullen.

"It feels like we're screwing with the Hawaiian spirits. This is bad. What should we do?" he said.

"I don't know," I told him.

"Bless the maintenance building," someone suggested.

● ● ● ● ●

Kawaiāhaʻo Church and buildings had a mystique about them that sent chills down my spine late at night if I was sent there for some reason. During the day, it was a grand place to visit. The old church embodies a past culture that speaks of a more gracious time, a time less hectic. The old buildings on the grounds echo this sentiment, particularly the mission houses, which provide a brief glimpse of what life was like when the monarchy still existed. All the officers in Sector Seven had an opportunity to visit the old church and grounds for one reason or another. Most of the time it was in response to an entry alarm.

One extremely busy night on the first shift an alarm call came in for the Kawaiāhaʻo preschool. The only officer available was Mike, who arrived on the scene fairly quickly. A few minutes later he was calling for another officer.

"One-six-nine to four-seven, what do you have there?"

"Sarge, come by."

"Whatcha got?"

"Sarge, just come by."

Kawaiāhaʻo Church is located at the intersection of King and Punchbowl streets.

I was more than curious by now. Mike sounded very serious, and he never sounded very serious. When I arrived a few minutes later, Mike was parked just inside the Punchbowl gate near the front doors of the church. As I got out of the car, Mike was already speaking.

"Do you hear that?"

"What?"

"The music."

I listened and heard what sounded like the final chords of a musical piece. Then it was quiet.

"Yeah, I thought I heard some music," I said.

"It's coming from inside the church," Mike said.

The church was dark. Mike said that when he arrived he went to the preschool and checked all the doors and windows. Everything was locked. As he was finishing, he heard music playing. He drove to the front and listened to what, according to him, was unmistakably music, coming from inside the church. Mike and I walked around the building and checked for a possible entry. Everything looked okay. If I hadn't heard a few seconds of music myself, I would have blamed Mike for pulling another one of his pranks. We called for a caretaker to come down, and in about a half hour, we were checking inside the church. Again, everything was okay.

The caretaker locked up, and we walked away toward our cars.

"I didn't hear anything," Mike said rather pensively.

"Okay, I didn't hear anything either," I said.

• • • • •

Just across from the church on Mission Lane are the restored mission houses. Because of their historic value, the old homes have alarms to indicate unauthorized entry. Late one night on the first shift, we got a call about an alarm there. We arrived in a few minutes and parked on Mission Lane. A representative from the alarm company was already there, and informed us that their system was showing an entry. We found the houses to be locked tight. Every door and window was closed and locked.

The old mission houses, viewed from the King Street side

The alarm company guy was puzzled. The system showed an entry for the house farthest from Mission Lane, but everything was locked.

"Okay, let's go inside and check," I suggested.

The company representative unlocked the house, and we entered. It was the first time I had been inside one of the houses, and even though we were searching in the dark with our flashlights, I was fascinated by all the antique furniture, artifacts, and clothing. We carefully searched everything and everywhere. I was amazed at how close the ceiling was to our heads and how small and steep the stair steps were. As we walked through the rooms, I tried to imagine what it would have been like to live in those cramped quarters. Everything looked undisturbed, and I was glad no one had violated the sanctity of that historic landmark. We walked outside and stood talking to the company representative.

"You must have some kind of system failure," I told him. "We'll make checks of the buildings for the rest of the night, but you probably need to have someone check the house during the day."

The alarm man was reluctant to agree, because a diagnostic test of the system showed it to be working properly. We cajoled him into locking the door and having the staff at the alarm company reset the alarm. For a few minutes all was well; then the company reported an entry again. The alarm company man with us unlocked the door and opened and closed it a couple of times, as if the electronic problem would go away.

"Yeah, maybe you're right. We gotta look at the system," he said as he was lighting up a cigarette.

We were preparing to leave when the alarm man began to shout loudly and point to a window upstairs.

"Look! Look! Look!" he shouted.

"What?"

"There was a guy in the window looking down at us."

We all looked up at the window he was pointing to. There was no one in the window, but if he said he saw someone, then we needed to search the interior of the old home once more. There was no reason to disbelieve the alarm guy. We surely could have missed a suspect who was well hidden inside. We again conducted a room-by-room search of the old house, this time with two officers side-by-side to ensure we missed nothing and to provide backup if we found the suspect. Make that *when* we found the suspect. We left the alarm representative outside to watch the door to make sure no one fled as we searched. Room by room we found nothing. We stopped frequently to stand quietly in the dark, listening for the sound of any movement. There was nothing. We completed our search and then searched again. Nothing.

We left the house and stood outside. Each of us occasionally glanced up at the window pointed out earlier by the alarm representative. Everyone was uncomfortable. We conducted the most thorough search we could. We found no one.

"Could there be, like, hidden doors, or something?" one of the officers asked.

The alarm company representative shrugged. He was feeling uncomfortable, too.

"I don't like this I don't like this," Mitch was muttering, as his eyes scanned the building.

"Okay, well, we're leaving. We gotta get back on the road. Call us if you need anything." I politely offered to the alarm man.

We were almost to our cars on Mission Lane when the alarm man began shouting again.

"Come! Come! Come! There's somebody inside!"

We ran back to the house. The alarm man was pointing to the window again. It was open.

"Did somebody open the window?" I shouted to my men, as my own level of apprehension soared. No one had opened the window.

"Open the door!" I called to the alarm man.

We searched the house again. We looked under beds, we looked in closets, we looked behind furniture, we looked in cabinets—and we even looked in some of the drawers that could be opened. In fact, everything that could be opened was opened. We poked around the cellar for trap doors; there weren't any. We pushed on walls and on the ceiling for loose boards. There weren't any. I asked if there was a possible passage between the two houses, a tunnel—something? The alarm man said he didn't know.

It had been nearly two hours since we first arrived at the house. We locked up the site, made a last check of the exterior, and gathered one last time in front.

"The company shows another entry," the alarm man stated.

"It's a malfunction," someone replied.

We walked back to our cars. No one dared to look up at the windows.

• • • • •

The last time I was on the grounds of Kawaiāha'o Church was in response to yet another alarm at the preschool building. We went in a group—for obvious reasons. We walked slowly, and one of the officers turned the handle of each door as we passed to ensure that all were locked. They were. When we reached the end of the building, we turned around to go back.

All the doors we had just checked and found to be locked were ajar.

• • • • •

It has been many, many years since I visited Kawaiāha'o Church and its grounds, but in 1999, while Christmas shopping at Aloha Tower Marketplace with my family, I came across an antique slate roof shingle from the church. It was recovered some years back when the church was reroofed. An artist had carved a petroglyph-like figure onto it. A man, a woman, and two children. The old shingle was now a work of art.

It has more meaning for me than people know. It probably clung to the roof of the church and watched us twenty-five years ago as we waited in hiding for the kid who was turning on the water sprinklers. Or when we frantically searched that mission house for the face in the window. Or when we wanted to run away because all the locked doors swung open behind us in the preschool.

And now it's hanging in my house.

23
Kaka'ako Sniper

"Dispatch . . . forty-seven, a man with a rifle on the rooftop parking of eight-seven-five Waimanu Street."

It was 8:25 in the morning on March 9, 1979. Callers were telling HPD dispatchers that a male was on the roof of a self-storage building, holding a rifle. He wasn't threatening anyone; he was just displaying it. We arrived within a few seconds of each other. Mike, Roy from Sector Eight, Kaui, and I met at the spiral ramp leading to the parking area. From confirmations on the radio, I knew other officers were responding. When we arrived, the man was hanging the rifle over the rooftop wall at the mauka–Diamond Head corner.

"Stay here. Watch him. Let us know if he moves. When the other officers arrive, put someone from Sector Eight at the ramp, then come up with the others," were the instructions I gave Kaui.

We drove up the ramp of the multistory storage facility. Roy led the way, Mike followed, and I brought up the rear.

The rooftop was a large rectangle, with parking stalls along the perimeter walls and a row of stalls down the middle. Almost directly in the middle, at the point where the ramp entered the roof landing, was a large air-conditioning intake/exhaust structure. At the mauka-'Ewa corner was a wall-and-glass room containing the building's elevator.

There were no transmissions from Kaui until we reached the roof. "He just disappeared from view," she reported.

When we reached the top, Roy and Mike turned right toward the suspect's last known position. I went left, in case he had moved in that direction. I stopped about twenty feet from the ramp, grabbed my portable radio, and started to get out of my car. I heard nothing from Roy or Mike. Then it started.

BOOM!

It sounded like a cannon going off. Actually, the shot was echoing off the cement walls of the building and probably sounded louder than it actually was. I stumbled and lost my footing. I crashed into the driver's side window of a parked car a few feet away with so much force that the window shattered. A woman was sitting behind the wheel of that car, and whether she thought she was being shot at or what, I don't know, but she started screaming.

"He's shooting!" I shouted into my portable radio. "Get us some help up here."

BOOM! came another shot from the Diamond Head side of the parking lot. I ran to a group of cars near the air-conditioning unit and called on my radio to Mike or Roy. There was no response. BOOM! Another shot. In a crouch, I worked my way through the parked cars toward the ramp that led to the suspect. From this new position, I could see Roy's car. His windshield was shattered. I couldn't see Roy. I thought the worst. I moved to my right, toward Mike's car, and saw Mike crouching at the right rear of his car.

BOOM! Part of the rear corner of his car exploded into jagged pieces that resembled metallic popcorn. The bullets were piercing and exploding through the thin metal sides of his car. I was about to shout at him to get out of there, but he didn't need prompting. From a crouched position, Mike jumped and ran to the safety of the concrete wall of the ramp. I eased myself up over the trunk of a car to get a look. The suspect was standing behind a car in the mauka–Diamond Head corner of the roof, holding the rifle at shoulder level. He saw me and swung the rifle in my direction. BOOM! The windshield of a car to my right exploded, and I could hear more glass shattering behind me.

I realized that if he zeroed in on one of us with his scope, there was nothing we could do.

"Roy!" I shouted. No response.

"Mike!" I called. "You and I alternately return fire." I wanted to see if returning fire would keep the suspect pinned down. I watched Mike rise and BOOM! the wall in front of him exploded into dust, and bits of concrete flew in every direction. I rose and barely had time to level my gun when BOOM! the man fired at me. I felt the concussion with the change of air pressure and heard the shrill, screaming whistle as the bullet passed very close to my head. The moment was brief, but sobering. I watched Mike rise again and drop back down without shooting as another bullet flew in his direction.

I could hear voices coming over the radio from officers below us on the roadway, telling dispatch there was shooting on the roof.

"Dispatch, we're pinned down!" I shouted into the portable radio. "We need more help up here."

"Ten-four, one-six-nine, we have officers on the way, and SWAT has been notified," came a calm and controlled voice. It was instantly annoying. Strangely, I found myself becoming angry with her. *How could she be so damn calm at a time like this?*

I turned my attention back to the suspect. I peered over the trunk of another car. I couldn't see him. It had been quiet for a minute. Was he still in the corner? Did he move? Seconds later, a woman rose from behind a car and began running toward Mike. The suspect stood up. BOOM! The woman fell screaming. I stood up, and he turned toward me. BOOM! BOOM! I flung myself against a car, still unable to aim my gun at him. I tried to find the woman again, but she had crawled under a car and disappeared from my view. She was screaming. I feared she had been shot. Later, I would learn I was right.

"My wife is down there!" came a shout from behind me. A man coming out of the elevator room started running down the ramp. I reacted without thinking. I jumped up and ran to him, grabbing him by the shirt and pulling him down. I turned to see the suspect pointing his rifle directly at me. His head was canted toward the gunstock, and I clearly understood that he was looking through his scope. I saw the puff of smoke and felt the air whistle beside my head as the bullet screamed by. Concrete fragments struck me on the back of my head and neck. I threw myself to the ground. I was terrified, and I was furious at the man on the ground next to me. In order to prevent him from being hurt or killed himself, I had to expose myself clearly to the shooter. It was the first time during the incident that I thought I might die. I grabbed the man by the back of his neck and shouted at him, "Stay behind the f—kin' wall." I half crouched and crawled back to the air-conditioning unit.

My head was pounding, and I was becoming confused and distressed. Too many things were adding to the confusion and interfering with our ability to concentrate on the shooter: not hearing from Roy and thinking he was shot, the woman falling to the ground and screaming, the guy running in the lane and shouting for his wife, the bullets coming so close to my head.

It seemed as if many, many minutes had passed since the shooting began, and still I had no additional officers on the roof to help. I knew that Kaui was downstairs and other officers should have been a mere minute away, yet no help came. Mike was pinned down behind the ramp wall. I moved from car to car, looking for a position from which I could return fire. I still worried that Roy had been shot and was either dead or in desperate need of help. The situation was looking very bad.

Then I heard a SWAT unit officer report that he was responding. It was Joe, a good friend from my District Four days. I grabbed my portable radio.

"Joe, we need you up here. This guy's got us pinned down real good."

"Hang on. I'll be there shortly."

The shooting had pretty much stopped since the gunman fired at me on the ramp, and I had time to catch my breath. Suddenly a car appeared at the top of the ramp, and I saw the blue light on its roof. Finally, help was here. It was Jimmy, a relief officer in our district. He got out of his car, and I shouted the gunman's location to him.

BOOM! The suspect fired in our direction. Jimmy looked at me with a wide grin and said, "This is just like on TV." Then he ran forward and threw himself on the ground at the front of Mike's car. Before I could say anything, he began shooting at the suspect. He let go four or five shots.

BOOM!

"God! I'm shot!" cried Jimmy. Then he stood up in plain view of the suspect, grasping his hand. I realized that if the shooter wanted to, he could have killed Jimmy right at that moment.

Jimmy turned toward me; he was about fifteen feet way. His face was splattered with blood and fragments of bone and flesh. His uniform shirt was also covered in blood. My eyes went to his palm, which was spurting blood. His fingers were torn and splayed in unnatural positions.

There was no question now about someone getting hurt. One of the men under my command was shot. The blood was real, the mangled hand was real, the pain was real, the terror was real. I had to think about Jimmy.

"Jimmy, go to Mike! Go to Mike! Mike, take him down the ramp!" I shouted, and grabbed my radio.

"One-six-nine! We have an officer shot!"

"One-six-nine, repeat your last."

"We have an officer shot!" I was screaming into the radio.

Mike grabbed Jimmy, and the two of them disappeared down the ramp.

At that moment, I never felt more alone in my entire life. Mike and Jimmy were gone. I thought Roy was dead or injured. No one else had come to help. My thoughts went to my two young sons, and for a moment I wondered if I would see them again. Things were beginning to look hopeless.

"I have a shot at the suspect, can I take it?"

I couldn't believe my ears. It was Roy. He somehow made it back to his car.

"Shoot the son-of-a-bitch!" I was beyond caring about my demeanor as I shouted into the radio.

"Negative! Negative! Don't shoot!" came a voice over the radio. "Don't shoot!"

I recognized the detective's voice, but I couldn't understand why he was countermanding my order. Where the hell was he, and why was he interfering with my decision?

BOOM! BOOM!

More shots. Now what? I couldn't see the suspect, I couldn't see Roy. I moved around the cars to find a better spot. Several minutes went by, and then I heard Roy again.

"I have him. He threw down his rifle, I have him."

I looked out and saw Roy standing over a man who was cuffed behind his back. On the ground next to them was a 30.06 rifle with a scope. I walked up to Roy.

"He shot Jimmy."

Roy's face drained. "I didn't know. Sarge, I didn't know." Roy believed that perhaps he could have shot the suspect before Jimmy was shot.

Suddenly the roof was crawling with police officers. My anger quickly returned.

"Where the hell were you guys when we needed you?"

I was venting all the anger and frustration and stress of the last twenty-two minutes. It had lasted only twenty-two minutes, but it seemed like two hours. My body hurt. My legs were weak. My head was pounding. We found the woman who was shot. The bullet passed through her purse, was deflected, and ripped out of the bag, injuring her hand and fingers. Besides her and Jimmy, no one else was injured.

The suspect was kept on his stomach as officers began to preserve the scene. Soon after, he was taken down the ramp to the street below. Then the Homicide Detail lieutenant appeared on the roof. My heart sank. In the instant that I saw him, I wondered if Jimmy had been shot in the chest as well as the hand and had died. But he assured me that Jimmy was at Queen's and the doctors were working on him. Homicide was there because the CID major wanted the most experienced detail on the case.

Kaui came out of a stairwell while I was talking to some other officers. She looked devastated. I suppose I didn't look like a welcoming committee either.

"What happened? Where were you guys?" I asked angrily.

"The CID major refused to let us come up. We tried to find a stairwell or something. We couldn't find a way up."

My anger shifted to the CID major. Didn't he realize how many lives could have been lost because of his refusal to allow help to go up to the roof? I wasn't sure how to handle this. Somehow, we muddled through that day and the next and the next and very slowly returned to normal.

During the weeks and months after the shooting, we were depressed and had difficulty sleeping. Some of us felt detached and estranged from our responsibilities. We didn't know it then, but we were suffering from Post-Traumatic Stress Disorder, or PTSD. PTSD is a psychiatric disorder that can occur following the experience or witnessing of life-threatening events such as the sniper incident. One of the ways to alleviate the symptoms of PTSD is an immediate diffusing of the incident after the traumatic event. We know today that such diffusing therapy is critically important as a first step toward protecting against PTSD. This can be accomplished through a Crisis Intervention and Support Detail or Team that responds directly to the scene and is involved from the very start. This group is equivalent to a Peer Support Team, but usually has the benefit of having psychological therapists as team members.

One major deficiency of the department during those years was that there was no Crisis Intervention and Support Detail or Peer Support Group for officers who were involved in traumatic incidents. One possible result of unattended PTSD is burnout. PTSD victims feel useless and unproductive. They feel trapped in a condition that's not improving. Attitudes toward work are affected, and these victims stop caring anymore about their jobs and about their performance. In the long run, other people forget the incident that brought on the PTSD and look upon these victims as lazy and unproductive. They get bypassed for promotions and special job assignments. They may even be disciplined for their current behavior, with no thought as to the "why" behind it. The development of Peer Counseling and Crisis Intervention teams has gone a long way to prevent burnout.

In my case, I felt particularly vulnerable during that time because an officer was seriously injured in the shooting and I was the supervisor. Jimmy's hand lost flesh, nerves, and bone. Even though he underwent reconstructive surgery, his hand was permanently maimed and he eventually had to leave the department, taking a civilian position in the Records Division. For a very long time, I felt responsible for the entire incident, second-guessing myself that there might have been something I could have done differently to prevent the injuries that occurred. Perhaps I would not have had such a difficult time recovering had there been primary psychological support available in the form of a Crisis Intervention Team.

The department did conduct a formal critique of the incident a week or so after it occurred. Mike, Roy, and I were required to attend, since we played important roles in the incident. Many of the department's administrators were present. It was a particularly difficult meeting. The purpose of the critique was to identify what went right and what went wrong. It was a multihour session that forced us to relive the shooting almost minute-by-minute.

The meeting started with our reenactment of the shooting using photos and diagrams. The follow-up investigators provided their portion of the case, and the reenactment ended with a status report on the injured persons. Then the session was opened to questions and answers. One of the key questions asked was, "Why didn't all the officers return fire?" The answer was simple. We didn't have the opportunity. The shooter effectively had us pinned down. Several of the administrators simply couldn't understand our response. They couldn't understand how one shooter could pin down three officers. I was angry at their inability to see how difficult those twenty-two minutes were. In hindsight, I suppose those administrators never had the opportunity to be shot at and experience firsthand how difficult it is to use a .38 caliber handgun against a 30.06 rifle with a scope, at fifty yards no less.

Another question was, "Why didn't any of the officers at the scene have rifles?" Easy answer. The department does not provide rifles to any of the patrol officers, and none of us owned one. A much more difficult question was, "Did the officers at the scene follow policy and procedures?"

In our corner during the inquiry was Assistant Chief John Pekelo. He was a tall, big man known as "Big John," an administrator who came "from the trenches" and never forgot that fact. If we did the best we could, he supported us. He was also known for his gruff side, and the fact that he took no bullshit. John Pekelo asked me an important question.

"Dias, when the shooting started, what was your primary objective?"

I felt my throat and chest tightening. It was all coming down to the self-doubt that had been nagging me all week. *Was there something else I could have done?* I answered the best I could.

"When he began shooting, we needed to contain him, to keep him from moving about and shooting at more people. We needed to keep the threat confined in that corner of the roof. It became obvious very quickly that we were outgunned. The best course of action appeared to be to keep him where we could see him. If an opportunity arose to return fire and shoot him to prevent more injuries, we were prepared for that. But that opportunity never came up." *When the opportunity finally arose, Roy was ordered not to shoot by the detective.*

"Good enough for me," Pekelo responded. "Anybody got a problem with that?"

No one spoke. Some people thought we should have shot and killed the shooter. The fact is, we didn't have that opportunity. I have stated many times in the course of discussing this case that if the shooter really was trying to commit "suicide by cop" I would have been more than happy to oblige him, if he had given me the opportunity.

The critique session concluded that the officers on the rooftop did everything in their power to contain the suspect, minimize injuries to other officers and civilians, and bring the sniper incident to a close without further injuries to anyone, including the suspect.

Someone brought up the intervention by the detective when he heard Roy ask for permission to take a shot at the suspect. Everyone agreed that the detective's intervention was wrong. He wasn't at the scene and had no way to judge the circumstances that prompted Roy's question or my response. The detective himself, to his credit, acknowledged that he should not have countermanded my order. He later apologized personally to me.

That Roy even asked for permission to fire his weapon and that the detective so quickly tried to prevent an officer from shooting at someone underscored the department's culture of limited use of our guns. The underlying belief was that if we began to use our guns more, to mimic mainland departments, we would lose our reputation of being a nonviolent city in which the police are helpers and greeters and advisers, not gun-toting rangers and deputies who look for gunfights. Others feared that officers would develop an increased dependency on the use of guns. All agreed that officers department-wide needed to understand that when conditions called for the use of their handguns, and if they used them properly and according to law, they would not be in jeopardy, they would not be ostracized, and they would be supported by the department administrators.

The patrol major, who led the critique, wanted to bring the session to a close and asked if anyone had any other comments. One lieutenant raised his hand.

"With all due respect to everyone at the incident, I wish to point out that Sergeant Dias did not follow protocol and procedures in his use of the radio. He was shouting, and in one instance he used profanity."

This was just too much for Pekelo. His deep voice boomed across the room.

"Shut up and sit down, you damned fool. If someone was shooting at you with a high-powered rifle you would shout and swear too. You want to talk anymore about radio demeanor, you come into my office and do it."

The meeting was over.

Several months later, Mike, Roy, Jimmy, and I were each awarded the Bronze Medal of Valor, the department's third-highest award, for minimizing bloodshed and bringing the sniper incident to a successful ending. The suspect was convicted of four counts of attempted murder and sentenced to four life terms with the possibility of parole.

The case was over. But the events of that day have lingered on in my life for much too long.

24
Discretion

Have you ever been stopped by a police officer for driving in some fashion that violates the traffic code? As you sat waiting for him to come up to your car did you wonder if he'd be nice enough to give you a warning? There actually are some things you can do to increase your chance that the cop will give you a warning instead of a citation. Here are a few rules to follow when stopped by the nice police officer.

1. Don't call out, "Whaaat? What I did?"
2. Even though you're secretly hoping the cop is suffering from a bad case of rash in places he won't even show his wife, do say, "Good morning" or "Good evening." Pleasantly.
3. Acknowledge your guilt early—even though you're absolutely certain you were only doing thirty-five coming down Pali Highway. Of course, you know that absolutely no one does thirty-five coming down Pali Highway.
4. After saying, "I'm sorry," say that you will "be more aware of your speed." Don't say you'll never do it again. We all know that as soon as the cop leaves you'll be speeding.
5. When you feel like challenging his observation that you violated the law, see rule 3. Particularly, never say, "How could you tell from your position? Huh? Huh?"
6. Praise his choice of dark glasses. A suggestion is, "I like your glasses. Where did you get them?" Stop there. Do not add, "Longs?"
7. Never say, "Hurry up, I gotta be at a meeting in ten minutes."
8. It is permissible to try the claim, "I was speeding 'cause I really gotta go bathroom."

9. Cry. And say, "My husband is going to hit me *again* when he finds out about this." This rule has been shown to be very effective in changing the tag to a warning. Male motorists may use this rule, but should say, "My wife . . . " instead of "My husband . . . ." But don't hold your breath.

10. If you're brave enough to say, "I'll see you in court," you will.

Police discretion is founded in the belief that people don't always intend to commit a crime or violate the traffic code. We all make mistakes. Police officers' girlfriends, boyfriends, spouses, sisters, brothers, dads, moms, and kids make mistakes, and we all hope for a break in those cases. So society tells law enforcement that police officers should be allowed to use their discretion and make judgments based on mitigating or aggravating circumstances.

There is a clear difference between the concepts "the letter of the law" and "the spirit of the law." Enforcing "the letter of the law" means enforcing the specifics of the law without exception. Take murder, for example. It would be totally inappropriate for a homicide detective to say to his lieutenant, "Boss, the guy was Joe's third cousin on his mother's side, why don't we just look the other way this time?"

On the other hand, there may be a societal need to have specific laws on the books, but society wants police officers to make judgments about enforcing those laws because there may be valid mitigating circumstances. The classic example is the traffic citation. The community expects the officer to be mature enough and to have the proper training and development to take the best interests of the community into consideration when making discretionary judgments.

Of course, being related to or a friend of a police officer is also an important consideration. Remember the hiring interview question, "Would you tag your mother?" Never try a version of this excuse on a cop by using my name.

"Oh, Officer, you remember retired Major Dias? He's my good friend."

That could get you arrested, depending on who the cop is who stopped you.

Usually, discretion does not apply to the criminal side of the law, but there are times when society would be offended if we pursued certain cases. One example of this is a story I call "Aku Eye and the Potato."

One day when Tom Pickard was the receiving desk captain and I was the receiving desk sergeant, an officer brought in a shoplifting arrest from a major grocery chain. The "suspect" was an elderly Japanese woman. She had to be in her eighties. She was bent over and walked on crooked legs that had probably seen many years of hard work, and she looked traumatized to be in the receiving desk among all the officers. As we took custody of her, the officer went into Pickard's office to explain the arrest. The Juvenile Crime Prevention Division two hundred yards across the street probably heard the resulting explosion.

The woman was arrested by store security for stealing one, yes, you read that right, just one potato. She told the HPD officer who took custody of her that her husband was sick in bed and that they did not have any food. She did not take the potato for herself. She needed it for her husband. The store manager, however, told the HPD officer that shoplifting is shoplifting. They felt bad for her, but the law is the law, after all.

The HPD officer should have used his discretion and not brought the old woman into the desk to Captain Pickard.

Captain Pickard stormed out of his office, leaving the arresting officer behind. He looked at the old woman and smiled at her as he pulled up a chair.

"Mama," he asked, "your husband sick?"

The woman nodded. "I think he dying. He very weak. We no more food."

"Is that why you took the potato?"

The woman nodded again and tears fell from her eyes.

Pickard patted her on the back and stood up. He took a twenty dollar bill from his wallet and handed it to an officer.

"Take her with you, go buy her food, then take her home."

He pointed at me, his aku eye bulging.

"You call the Salvation Army, Catholic Charities—I don't know who, I don't care who—you find her help and someone who is going to follow up with her. Now!"

He looked at the arresting officer, who was feeling quite small.

"You, use your head next time. And don't you ever bring in an old woman who took a potato for her sick husband."

We bought her food and took her home. I found her help.

This incident brought home a statement made to me by my father on the day I graduated from recruit school: "Remember the little guy."

My dad worked all his life on the waterfront as a longshoreman and stevedore. He left intermediate school to help support his family. He knew what it was like to struggle to feed his kids. He knew what the word "sacrifice" meant to people who had very little money. When he told me to remember the little guy, I thought he meant to respect people. Aku Eye and the potato incident made the meaning of my father's words very clear. He was telling me not only to have respect for people who have little money and who are struggling, but also to have compassion as well. The compassion that Tom Pickard showed to that old woman burned into my mind. This was part of the great respect I have for him. That and the fact that his commonsense approach to police work reminded me of my father. I think if Dad had been aware of the concept, he would have told me that the spirit of the law is equally as, if not more important than the letter of the law. I think he would have said to temper action with respect and compassion and, if possible, to learn the "why" behind people's behavior.

Years after this incident, I began teaching courses on criminal justice, or criminology, at various colleges and universities in Honolulu. Inevitably, the topic of ethics and values arises, and I like to open the discussion with the question "What would it take for you to steal?" Initially, students usually claim that there is no condition that would force them to steal. Then I change the question just a little and ask, "Would you steal to feed your children?" To a person, each student answers, "Yes." Then I introduce the story of Captain Tom "Aku Eye" Pickard and the potato and begin a discussion on police ethics, values, and discretion.

So next time you're stopped by a police officer for speeding, try this:

"Good morning, Officer. I'm sorry; it was all my fault. And *say*, I like your glasses. Did you know I'm a friend of Gary Dias, and I really gotta go to the bathroom. [Start sobbing.] And, oh God, if you give me that ticket my wife is going to hit me again."

25
Time to Change Assignment

After the sniper incident in Kaka'ako, I needed a change. I needed to get away from patrol for a while. I submitted a request to transfer to the Criminal Investigation Division (CID). Within a few months I became a detective. It meant a different type of work, plain clothes, and a new badge.

The new assignment also meant I became the low man on the proverbial pole again. Sergeants and detectives hold the same rank at HPD. In some jurisdictions, the rank of detective is equivalent to that of a motor-patrol officer. In the CID, the detective is the lowest-ranking officer on staff.

CID handles the follow-up investigations for all felonies and some misdemeanors. Detectives are responsible for identifying suspects and presenting cases to the prosecutors for charges leading to trial.

The felony offenses committed in the community had respective CID details that were responsible for each class of offense. Each district on the island had a Burglary/Theft Detail. Other details were Forgery, Auto Theft, and White Collar Crime. Details that handled violent crime were Rape, Robbery, and Homicide. The General Detail handled assaults and miscellaneous cases. Each detail was headed by a lieutenant and had from six to eight detectives assigned to it. CID also had detectives working on evening and night shifts to handle arrests made during those hours. These shifts had their own lieutenants and were similar to the daytime General Detail.

I didn't realize it at the time, but the department was committing a terrible disservice to rookie detectives. Usually the people assigned to CID were experienced officers promoted to the rank of detective or experienced sergeants who were transferred to the position. And that was the source of the error. Administrators and commanders believed that since these officers were experienced, they would fit right in. Unfortunately, officers and sergeants outside CID had no real opportunity to handle follow-up investigations, develop the *corpus delicti* (elements of the crime), and charge suspects with offenses. In addition, most officers who testified in court did so as witnesses, not as lead investigators.

Back then, the department threw us in and hoped we'd learn quickly. There were no training sessions for new detectives. No classes on evidence. No courses on crime-scene investigation. And perhaps most important, no one taught us how to interview witnesses or interrogate suspects. We reported to work on our first day and immediately went into a rotation to be assigned cases. If we needed to learn how something was done, we asked a senior detective. And we hoped we asked the one who knew how it was done, not the one who guessed how it was done, and not the one who was lazy and recommended we not do it at all. If we weren't sure, we asked our lieutenant, but remember, the lower ranks of the department maintained a belief that we should not bother our supervisors—there were plenty of experienced people at our own rank who could offer advice.

So there I was, new man on the block, low man on the pole, not knowing which way was up. What I did know was that I was assigned to the night shift, and that we could be responsible for any type of felony investigation. I spent my first few hours learning procedures from other detectives who were willing to help. Others, who looked as if they were not so willing, were slamming away on typewriters typing up their investigations. It became obvious very quickly that detectives in CID were backlogged with cases.

I don't remember my first case. Or my first few weeks. I now attribute that loss of memory to the post-traumatic stress I was still suffering from the sniper incident. My self-esteem was really low at that point in my career, and although I didn't realize it then, it was good to be able to submerge myself in the investigation of criminal offenses. One case, though, does stand out.

One night I was sitting in the CID front office typing a case when my lieutenant came up.

"You got a theft-first case in Waikīkī."

A gentleman named Bob, from a small town in Kansas, was here at a convention. It was his first trip to Hawai'i. It was actually, he said, his first trip anywhere. To top it off, he was here alone. His company sent him to the convention, but he didn't have enough money to take his wife. She was disappointed, but they managed to scrape up some extra money so he could enjoy himself. He had worked long years, and the fruits of his labor were now paying off. He spent his days at the convention attending meetings and lectures and break-out group discussions. Then he went back to his hotel room and spent quiet evenings watching TV. He really didn't have that much money, and he felt guilty spending the extra money his wife gave him.

On his last night in Hawai'i, Bob decided to go for a walk along Kalākaua Avenue. He window-shopped for a while, walked into a few shops, and bought a few trinkets to take home for the family. Then Bob met Candice.

Candice was a young woman who worked evenings in Waikīkī. She too was walking Kalākaua Avenue. And she saw him coming. Something weakened in our tourist, and he stopped to talk to Candice. Perhaps he was lonely. Perhaps he enjoyed the compliment this young woman was paying him through her smile and touch on his arm. Perhaps Bob felt a neglected need for adventure and risk taking. Whatever it was, Bob made the mistake of stopping to talk to Candice.

Within a few minutes, Candice was suggesting that he enjoy the last night of his Hawai'i vacation with her. She would make him feel good and he would be able to sleep well before his long trip home in the morning. All for fifty dollars cash. No checks, no Visa, no MasterCard. Our tourist weakened even further and agreed to take Candice to his room just a few hotels away. After all, he had $280 cash in his wallet, and even after paying Candice he would still take home $230 to his wife. Apparently he didn't give any thought to anything else he might be taking home to his wife after an evening with Candice. He mentioned to me that he was giddy with excitement that this young woman thought him attractive. He mentioned to me that he never, quote, "used" a lady of the evening before, and he thought, so far away from home, what harm could possibly come of it?

So he took Candice to his room, and she unbuttoned his shirt and undid his belt buckle. And then came the hook. She told him that she could smell the worries and work of the day on him and would he mind taking a shower. Imagine that. The streetwalker asking the john to take a shower. That's a reversal of conditional requirements, if you ask me. But Bob eagerly agreed, and into the shower he jumped.

About a minute later, no more, he heard a door close. His door. He came out of the shower and looked into the room. His wallet was lying on the bed, Candice was gone, and so was his money. He grabbed a towel, just a towel, wrapped it around his waist and gave pursuit. Candice, perhaps through overconfidence, was standing at the elevator.

"STOP!"

Candice sprinted to the exit stairwell. Bob gave chase. He chased her down the stairwell into the hotel lobby. Here, Candice showed great ingenuity and began to shout.

"Help me! Stop him. He's chasing me."

Bob, trying to hold tightly onto his towel, also began to scream.

"Stop her. She took my money."

Hotel security, unable to decide at the moment which of them was telling the truth, joined in the chase, following Bob, who was following Candice. Candice was thirty years younger than Bob and was running full tilt. Bob, on the other hand, had the motivation of trying to explain the loss of all his money to his wife, and was doing fairly well for himself in spite of his age, weight, and two-pack-a-day cigarette habit.

Candice hit Kalākaua and decided she would lose her pursuers down a side street. Problem: Fourth Watch was on the road, and Candice ran into the waiting arms of a new recruit, who recognized her from the night before, when he had stopped her and submitted an interrogation card on her prostitution activities. Bob soon caught up, and the hotel security after him. According to the officer, the only one not breathing hard was Candice. Understandably. After all, she was accustomed to lots of nightly exercise. The stories were told, Candice was arrested, and Bob and the security officers were driven back to the hotel. I met with Bob, took his statement, and returned to the station. Before leaving, Bob did ask the classic question.

"Does my wife have to know about this?"

I tried my best to remember that stern Joe Friday look.

"No, sir."

Back at the receiving desk, I met up with Candice as she was being booked by Mrs. M., one of the matrons. I introduced myself and asked Mrs. M. if she had discovered any money in Candice's property. She said no and asked me why. I told her the entire story.

"I know where the money is," said Mrs. M.

"Where?" I asked.

Mrs. M. looked at me in astonishment.

"You know where."

"No, I don't." I really didn't.

"Gary, it's up there," she said with a jerk of her head.

"Up where?" I persisted.

"Inside her." Mrs. M. was becoming frustrated.

"Huh?"

"Come on," said Mrs. M., as she grabbed Candice by the arm and walked her to the women's bathroom. Thirty seconds later, Mrs. M. came out with a rolled-up wad of moist twenty-dollar bills.

"Where did you get that?" I asked.

"IN-SIDE-HER!"

"How the hell could she run with that up there?" I asked, baffled.

Mrs. M. just shook her head and held the bills out to me. I wasn't about to take them

"Can you do the evidence report, please?"

Mrs. M. just shook her head again and walked back into the bathroom. I was thrilled that we recovered evidence, and went back to CID to call Bob and tell him we recovered the money. He asked a good question. Was all of it there? I didn't know. I assumed it was all there, since Candice didn't have time to drop by Liberty House for a quick shopping trip or step out for a cold one as she was running from Bob. I needed to check with Mrs. M. She didn't remember. It was two hundred something, she said. She had completed the evidence report and it had already been picked up by the evidence room custodian.

At the evidence room counter, the custodian was counting the money. Every other bill, he licked his thumb. I opened my mouth to stop him, but it was too late. He was nearing the end of the count. He finished. I didn't have the heart to tell him where that wad of bills had come from or the road it had traveled before reaching his hands.

"How much do you have there?"

"Two-eighty."

"Thanks."

Candice was convicted. Then she appealed the case. And she won. The State Intermediate Court of Appeals overturned Candice's conviction on the basis that we violated her right against unreasonable search and seizure. In other words, we deprived her of her Fourth Amendment right. If you can't remember the Fourth Amendment, it goes like this:

The right of the people to be secure in their persons, houses, papers, and effects, against unreasonable searches and seizures, shall not be violated, and no Warrants shall issue, but upon probable cause, supported by Oath or affirmation, and particularly describing the place to be searched, and the persons or things to be seized.

Yup. We violated that right. An unreasonable search and seizure was committed by Mrs. M., with my consent, and under the authority of my investigation. Detectives assigned to a case, you see, are responsible for everything that happens in that case, including the bad stuff. So Candice's case was overturned, and I say with complete sincerity that our court system prevailed and did exactly what our forefathers wanted it to do more than two hundred years ago: protect our cherished personal rights.

Many years later, I was taking night classes at Chaminade in an effort to obtain a master's degree. One of the required classes was Constitutional Law. This particular class was taught by Carolyn Brown, a capable, experienced, and respected attorney who worked with the public defender's office. I had known Carolyn from my years as a detective and later as the homicide lieutenant. I remember that first night of class when Carolyn walked in and saw me.

"Gary!" she exclaimed. "Oh, I'm so glad you're in this class. One of the cases we're going to discuss is *Candice v. Hawai'i.* You can tell us firsthand all about it."

Oh joy, I thought. *I get to tell the class how I screwed up as a young detective and got my name into the legal journals that discussed court decisions and opinions.* But it turned out okay. Carolyn's class helped me gain a deeper understanding of just how important it is to preserve the personal rights that the framers of our Constitution fought the British for over two hundred years ago.

Our society got its rights preserved. Candice got to skate out of a criminal charge. Bob got back his $280. I got an A.

26
Burglary/Theft Detail

Within a few months of my transfer to CID, I found myself reassigned to a Burglary/Theft detail. The area of my squad's assignment was Punahou Street to Makapuʻu Lighthouse, from the mountains to the sea. My first assignment was the beat from ʻĀina Haina to Niu Valley. It was a busy area, and I found myself with new cases every day.

In 1979, in my area alone, there were anywhere from six to fifteen burglary and theft cases every day. We did not, however, investigate each and every one of them. We used a case management system to keep up with the workload in a way that made sense. Most of the cases had no leads, no evidence, and no witnesses. These dead-end cases went nowhere unless a suspect was arrested and subsequently confessed to those cases. Every morning, we went over our cases, identified those with no leads, and spoke to the complainants. If no other information was discovered through those telephone calls, we sent letters to the complainants identifying the detective, the report number, and other miscellaneous information, and filed the cases away.

The remaining cases had evidence that required further investigation. We interviewed witnesses and neighbors to gain insight into a case. We submitted the names of known burglars to the Identification Section to have their fingerprints compared with latent fingerprints recovered from the crime scene. (Years later, the department invested in an Automated Fingerprint Identification System [AFIS], and suspects' fingerprints could be compared automatically.) We also examined suspects' *modus operandi* (method of operation, or M.O.) for clues that a suspect or group of suspects might be responsible for more than one case.

In the mid-seventies, there was a burglar in Kāneʻohe who entered homes while the owners were asleep. Instead of using a flashlight, he burned matches. When a match neared his fingers, he blew out the flame and dropped the match onto the floor. (I make absolutely no reference here to any ethnic joke regarding a homemade flashlight.) Anyway, we caught that guy and he went to prison. In 1980, a similar series of cases occurred in Kāhala. Remembering the Kāneʻohe case, I called the Oʻahu Community Correctional Center (OCCC) and learned that the Kāneʻohe burglar had been paroled a few months earlier. What we didn't have in the Kāhala cases were latent fingerprints that matched those of our Kāneʻohe burglar. Still believing that our suspect was the same guy, we went to his house. I took a book of matches with me and tore about half of them out. I walked up to the door and rang the bell.

"Bruddah, howzit. I haven't seen you since we arrested you for the Kāneʻohe burglaries. Do you remember me?" I asked him, cordially.

"Oh, yeah, howzit?" he replied.

"You burglarizing houses again?" I asked.

"Oh, no, brah. I learned my lesson," he answered, with a look that ratted his lie out.

I smiled at him and held up the half-empty book of matches—the implication being that I found them at a crime scene.

Our bungling burglar hung his head.

"Yeah, was me in Kāhala and Pearl City. I should have used one flashlight."

Hey, no one accused him of being brilliant. We arrested him, and he confessed to all the match-light burglaries.

The life of a burglary/theft detective is no great adventure. It's a tedious trudge through every day. The most frequent offense is a property crime, and in many cases there are few clues. You come home and find the screen cut, louvers removed. Your stomach churns at the thought that some creep intruded into your most personal and private place. Your neighbors didn't see anything, and the police don't find any evidence. You inventory the things taken and give the list to the police. That's about it. The insurance company later tells you that everything you listed has depreciated so much that the set of golf clubs you thought was worth $800 is worth only $17.25. Oops, the bag has a tear—make that $9.50.

And you're bitter. You feel violated. Your life has been disrupted. Your property has been taken. And where the hell were the cops when you needed them? It's that perception thing again. The problem gets bigger for detectives, though. The first question the victims ask is, "Did you catch the crooks?" Another frequent question is, "Do you think I'll get my property back?" This is a time when tactfulness comes in handy. The realistic answer is "No." But that's not what the victimized homeowners want to hear. They expect the detectives to be successful. And many times we are.

We had a series of burglaries all over the Mānoa area, and for a few months we were at a loss as to how to solve them. Then one day an alert neighbor saw a man coming out of his neighbor's house and called 911. The arriving officers caught the thief hiding in a garage a few doors down from the burglarized house. Several of us worked the case, and in no time the crook was confessing to every crime he ever committed.

One way to confirm a confession is to conduct a reconstruction with the crook. Several detectives take him for a ride. Literally. We put him in our car and tell him to take us to the places he burglarized. He points out the victim's residence and we confirm that against our case log. We then ask the crook to confirm what he took and where he pawned the goods. Most crooks have a very good memory for that sort of reconstruction.

My partner Tommy and I took the Mānoa crook for a reconstruction ride. He was fairly honest with us about the places he burglarized. He had excellent recall, except for where he sold the stolen goods. As we drove past one house, the crook pointed it out.

"I hit that place about two weeks ago. Took some jewelry. I forget where I sold it."

It was not on our logs.

"You sure?"

"Yup. Get plenty steps to the house and had one dog in the backyard, but never bark."

The house was built on the side of a mountain, and there certainly were a lot of steps leading up from the stone garage. In the garage was a car with its trunk open and groceries waiting to be carried inside.

"I'll go check upstairs," I offered. The rock steps leading to the house were steep, and of varying widths and heights. They looked as if they were carved from the side of the mountain.

After climbing what seemed to be hundreds of steps, I reached the front door. It was propped wide open with a bag of canned goods. The door opened to a large living room with a beautiful wood floor. I knocked on the door and called, "Hello?" Then I heard a clicking sound. Suddenly, the biggest German shepherd I have ever seen ran out of the hallway and into the living room. His eyes got really big, and I swear I saw him smile. As in a cartoon, all four of his legs were trying to run on the slippery wooden floor, and I realized what the clicking sound was. I turned and began to take leaping bounds down the narrow, steep, and uneven stairs. Why I simply didn't just move the bag of canned goods and shut the front door, I'll never know. Bounding down the stairs, I had all the grace of a runaway train. Once I started I couldn't stop. Momentum had complete control of me. Perhaps momentum knew that the dog was catching up to me and wanted me to move just a little bit faster. I don't move all that fast to begin with, but I gotta tell you I was flying down those stairs.

"Start the car!" I yelled to Tommy as soon as I turned the corner and reached the street. As I sprinted to the car, I realized the dog was so close that I wouldn't have time to stop and open the door. All I could do was throw the upper half of my body into the open passenger window.

"Go! Go! Go!" I yelled, as the dog began to bite at my ankles and shoes.

Tommy had tears of laughter running down his face as he slowly drove off with the dog hanging on to my pants. The crook was laughing too, of all the insults! Behind me I heard a woman calling out, "Sweetie! Sweetie "

The dog stopped. Tommy stopped. The woman was annoyed.

"I don't let my dog out of the house onto the street. She's not that kind of dog."

"Lady, your dog chased me, I didn't let it out of the house."

"It's because you ran."

I wanted to tell her to consider herself lucky I didn't shoot her damn dog, but I thought better of it. Tommy and the crook were still laughing as I explained who I was and why I took her dog for a walk. Yes, she did have a burglary, but didn't report it because the police never catch the crooks anyway.

"Well, we caught this one," I answered sarcastically, wishing I could add, "So there!" We confirmed the burg and property taken and returned to the station, where Tommy and I met with the crook alone in an interview room.

"The deal's off," I told the burglar.

"Why? You can't do that!" he said.

"Yes I can, and it's because you laughed at me and the dog."

The thief looked at Tommy.

"Can he do that?"

"I'm afraid so."

"I will give you one opportunity to get the deal back."

"What?"

"Where did you sel the stuff you stole?"

He gave it up in a second. There truly is no loyalty among thieves. The story he gave us was that a woman in Kaimukī was running a fencing operation out of her house. He claimed that he sold stolen property there on the day he was arrested. This was our probable cause to get a search warrant.

We were able to hit the house in the late afternoon, and to our great delight and dismay, the house was filled with stolen goods. And

I mean filled. It looked like a warehouse. Every room, including the bathroom, had stacks of TVs, radios, VCRs, boxes of jewelry, bicycles, guns, coin collections, you name it. In addition, there were several stashes of marijuana and cocaine. Finding all these items meant that we needed a "piggy-back warrant." When we enter a site on a search warrant and find evidence of other offenses, we have to go back to the judge and get a warrant that authorizes us to legally recover the other goods. Some argue that it's okay to simply recover the additional items, but it's better to be safe than sorry when it comes to evidence of crimes.

It took us all night and several truckloads to recover and transport the evidence to HPD. The "fence" was a woman in her late fifties. She was grandmotherly looking, but her swearing would make a drunken sailor proud. She was arrested for theft and receiving stolen property, and for weapons and drug offenses.

The Burglary/Theft details were the training grounds for advancement into violent crime units such as Rape, Robbery, or Homicide. The dream of most detectives was to be selected to fill a vacancy in one of those elite details. My partner Tommy got himself promoted and transferred to Internal Affairs, the unit that investigated police officers.

"Hey, Gary, how would you like to come to Internal Affairs?" Tommy asked one day.

"You mean Infernal Affairs? No thanks."

"No, it's a good place to work. It's a difficult position, yes, but you would like it here."

"Tommy, thanks, but no. I'm waiting for an opening in Robbery Detail."

"You start next week."

"What?"

"We needed a name. I put yours in. The chief approved it."

"Tommy, I really don't want to go."

"If you don't come, I'll tell everyone about the dog in Mānoa."

And that's how I got to Internal Affairs.

27
Internal Affairs

Internal Affairs (IA) is the unit that investigates police misconduct. In the early eighties it was a small unit composed of two details, one to conduct investigations into allegations against officers, and the other to conduct inspections of the various divisions within the department. Internal Affairs detectives rotated assignments between the Investigations and Inspections details.

Contrary to what some people think, most police officers are not corrupt. Most perform their duties with a high degree of professionalism and compassion for the people in their communities. Contact with the police, however, usually comes at a bad time in people's lives. The traffic tag, for example, is the most common negative contact. And in the course of negative human contact, complaints are made, in spite of the most professional behavior an officer can display.

Normally, the Police Commission investigates complaints against on-duty officers, provided the complaint is made within thirty days of the alleged misconduct. IA investigates complaints made after thirty days, and complaints against off-duty officers.

In an effort to help divisions and individual officers maintain their professionalism, IA conducts annual inspections. These inspections include division operations, filing systems, and personnel. The individual inspections include uniforms, equipment, licenses and certifications, and in cases of motor-patrol officers, cars. What I hated most were the surprise inspections. Everyone knows when the annual inspections are going to be held, and most people prepare very well for these events. After all, if you knew that I was going to inspect you, your equipment, and your car next Tuesday, you would make sure you met all the inspection requirements. Naturally then, the department conducts unannounced inspections.

One day a fellow IA detective, Russell, and I were assigned to drive to all the country patrol districts and conduct unannounced inspections of a few officers in each district. I felt sick. No one liked IA detectives. The arrival of an IA detective in a district was the bad news of the month, and going to each district almost guaranteed that we would find discrepancies that district commanders would have to answer to.

In District Two (Central Oʻahu and the North Shore), we inspected officers in Waimea, Waialua, and Wahiawā. Each of the officers had discrepancies that needed to be reported to his command. After the inspections, we drove to the Wahiawā Station to file our report. As we were walking out, Russell saw the district's major, John Gerard, a big, likable man whom he knew personally, walk in the front door. The major did not look pleased at our presence. But did that stop Russell? Not for a second.

"Big John!" Russell called out. "What's wrong with your troops? Everyone we stopped had problems."

Major Gerard did not have hair on the top of his head. And he was a man of fairly light complexion. My heart stopped as I watched the top of his head turn bright red. I muttered, "See you in the car," and left as quickly as I could. It was a few minutes before Russell came out of the building, looking perplexed.

"Gee, what the hell got into him?" Russell said as he got into the car. "I wonder if he was upset at our unannounced inspection?"

"Ya think?"

Not all inspections have unhappy endings, but the entire purpose of these reviews is to find areas of operations, equipment, and personnel that are not up to standards. Most of the time, these substandard conditions are easily fixed. Most of the time.

As part of the annual inspection of the Criminal Investigation Division, Chief Doug Gibb was conducting his review of the troops in the patrol squad room. The detectives were all dressed up in coats and ties, and the chief was making his way through the ranks. When the chief stepped in front of each detective, the detective presented his handgun at port arms and the chief took it from the detective for a casual inspection. Each weapon was unloaded. Most of the time.

That day, however, the chief grabbed the weapon of an old-time detective and popped open the cylinder. A couple of bullets fell to the floor, but the remainder stayed in the cylinder. Rusted in the cylinder. Chief Gibb handed the weapon to the CID division commander and stepped to the next man. From our position about ten yards away, we watched as the veins in the division commander's neck pulsed furiously.

On the other side of the house, an IA investigation is similar to a criminal investigation in having a complaint, a victim, a "suspect," perhaps witnesses, and in some cases evidence. The investigator puts this information together and prepares a list of "findings." A difference is that the investigator does not come to a conclusion. The conclusion regarding the guilt or innocence of the accused officer is a decision left to higher departmental authorities. Another big difference is that the investigation need only prove a "preponderance of evidence" rather than guilt "beyond a reasonable doubt," as in a criminal case.

Harry was an employee of an alarm company in Honolulu. He was also a thief. His scam was simple, yet seemingly brilliant. Harry used his authority and his access to keys to clients' businesses to enter the establishments after hours, steal goods, then set off the alarm and make the scene look as if a burglary had occurred. He was always the first on the scene. Harry didn't discriminate. He stole from all sorts of businesses, from golf and sporting goods stores to grocery stores and warehouses. The items he stole were also varied. Tires, rims, stereos, sound systems, golf clubs and bags, and food were all among the items he lifted during his nighttime escapades.

The brilliant part of Harry's scheme was to involve police officers. He did this by preying upon some officers' notion that they are underpaid and therefore entitled to free or cheaply priced services and items. Harry offered those officers whom he trusted the opportunity to buy things at a very low cost—for example, fifty dollars for a set of brand new golf clubs and bag. He provided food and drink for the softball games that officers played after work. And he gave things away. The number of officers receiving free items grew, and his circle of police contacts grew. Then one day, he got caught.

Harry was not a stupid person. He had been in prison before and he knew the rules. He knew that if caught he would go back to prison for a long time. He also knew that if he offered up police officers who were involved with him, he might receive a lighter sentence from the prosecution and courts. So he named officers and tied them to thefts and stolen property. Within days, the investigation blew wide open, and many officers were under scrutiny. Statement after statement was taken. Every one of the officers expressed shock at discovering that Harry was actually giving or selling them stolen property. Each one returned the property received.

This case illustrates the definition of the term "corruption." Corruption is "receiving money, or money's worth, to do something, or not do something that you would have been obligated to do or not do anyway." Taking the property from Harry for free or at a cheap price could be construed as payment for looking the other way or not properly investigating the suspicious circumstances under which Harry came to possess the property. Quite a few officers were disciplined for their involvement in this case, and one was fired.

Gratuities also fall under this concept of corruption. There are many opinions about the proper definition of *gratuity*. The department says that officers shall not accept gratuities. What about that cup of coffee or sandwich that the fast-food restaurant offers free at closing time? That puts the officer at the establishment as the business is counting money and sending employees into a darkened parking lot. Usually, the restaurants throw away the remaining food anyway. So is that corruption? Some argue that the officer, held to a higher standard than other people, should not accept any gratuity— that perhaps the free cup of coffee could lead to a free meal, then to a free hotel room, and the expected gratuities become greater and greater. And the businesses who offer the gratuities may expect and sometimes receive better police service than the businesses who don't. Others argue that it's the restaurant owners' right to offer free coffee to whomever they want.

The Harry incident hurt the department and the community when it occurred. The news media got hold of the investigation, and the rumors and gossip raged. The chief was hard put to convince the media and the community that the department was not covering up anything.

It is terribly difficult for a community to trust again when a police agency is found to have widespread corruption. Sometimes police officers are accused of maintaining a "code of silence." Most police officers, however, take their roles in the community seriously, strive to be professional, and refuse to be identified with corrupt officers.

The media play a big role in the issue of "cover-up" and trust. In 1988, after confessing to the murder of her husband, then–State Representative Roland Kotani, Grace Kotani committed suicide in a police headquarters restroom. She claimed that she needed to use the restroom because she was menstruating. Using this ruse, Grace took a sanitary napkin bag from her purse—which was in the possession of a detective—entered the bathroom, and shot herself in the head. The weapon she used was a .357 Magnum revolver hidden in the sanitary napkin bag.

In subsequent interviews with the media, a department spokesperson identified the gun as a .357 Magnum, but refused to show the weapon to the media. As good media people should do, some of them went straight to the nearest gun shop and asked to see a .357 Magnum handgun. The gun dealer was eager to oblige and showed them a .357 Magnum target gun with an eight-inch barrel— a gun that looked like a cannon and could not possibly have been hidden in Grace's bag without being noticed by the detective. The media asked the only question possible: what were we covering up?

One reporter even suggested that the police murdered Grace Kotani because she knew of a campaign smear her husband may have been involved with. But there was no cover-up. The weapon Grace used was a snub-nosed .357 revolver with a two-inch barrel. It would have been bad precedent to allow media to photograph evidence in a death case—or any case for that matter.

When police agencies become so rigid that they always conduct business behind closed doors, the community may begin to think local cops have forgotten they are a part of the community, not apart from the community, to paraphrase Sir Robert Peel.

We had a tight-knit group in IA and easily depended on each other for support in our investigations and inspections. My old beat partner Tommy, who was now our lieutenant, helped to keep us sane with his easy style and sense of humor. Life as an IA detective meant that many other police officers thought we were the enemy. When we walked into a division and people said, "Welcome," or "Good to see you," we knew they were lying. The IA detective did not forebear good tidings. Tommy realized that and allowed us moments of play when work was slow. One time we convinced the janitor to give us all the plastic bags of shredded paper so we could stuff a partner's office from wall to wall and floor to ceiling. Another time we lowered Russell's chair to its lowest position after he left for the day. When he came in the next morning, a woman was waiting to file a complaint with him against another officer. He invited her into his office and offered her a seat. It was too late for us to intervene. Russell sat, fell three-quarters of the way to the floor, and calmly looked up at the woman with his chin at the level of his desktop. Then with the greatest aplomb and coolness of character he asked the woman, "How may I help you?"

One day, another partner came to work to find a big wooden key hanging on his door.

"What's this?" he asked.

Tommy came out of his office holding a report the detective submitted the day before.

"That's the key to the John Deere," Tommy said, handing the report back to the detective.

"The key to what?"

"I couldn't make heads or tails out of your report, so I gave you the key to the John Deere tractor, to help you pull your head out of your ass."

From that day forward, we all waited for our turn at ownership of the key to the John Deere. And none of us was disappointed.

28
One Bad Ass

One day Tommy informed everyone that we would be working late, and that we were to report to the chief's office at 1700 hours, after most of the day-shift people left. What was up?

"Can't tell you," he said, teasing us into an even greater curiosity.

At 1700 sharp, we were all at the chief's door.

"Come in," called Chief Gibb.

As we sat around his desk, the chief told us that cheating on a police recruit exam was suspected, involving the entire class and perhaps the instructor. All the recruits were coming to the main station to be interviewed by IA detectives. Because recruits were not protected by the union, the chief decided that any recruit who refused to cooperate would be summarily dismissed. So would any recruit found to have cheated on the exams. We were also to try to learn what involvement, if any, the recruit lieutenant had in the alleged cheating. The chief then presented us with a typed order that we were to read to each recruit at the start of each interview. It notified the recruits that they were ordered to cooperate with the investigation. If they did not, their employment would be terminated.

When the recruits arrived, they were escorted to our offices one at a time. I was into my third or fourth interview when one young male recruit came into my office. I was tired and not amused that I was now into my third hour of overtime with the prospect of three more hours looming. I may have sounded a bit gruff.

"Sit down there."

I produced my notepad and began taking biographical data on the recruit. I may have glanced at him once. Then I read from the prepared statement given to us by the chief. As I got to the part about termination if the recruit was uncooperative, I noticed that the air in the room turned for the worse. *Gee,* I thought, *this guy is cutting loose.* I looked up to see the recruit sitting at attention, his face contorted and stretched into a wide grimace. I got scared.

"What's wrong?"

"Sir, I gotta go to the bathroom, sir."

"Go! For God's sake."

The recruit sprinted from my room and I slowly walked out. Tommy looked at me.

"What happened?"

"He had to go to the bathroom."

"Huh?"

"He had to go to the bathroom."

The IA inspector Hartwell Doane, saw the running recruit and came out of his office.

"What's going on?"

"Dias scared the shit out of that recruit," Tommy told him.

I protested to no avail. The inspector watched the front door to IA slowly close on its hydraulic hinge after the recruit ran out toward the nearest bathroom. Inspector Doane turned to me.

"Dias, you one bad ass," he said with a totally serious face. He walked back into his office as Tommy, laughing, handed me the keys to the John Deere.

After about two years of IA, I decided it was time to try to get promoted. I took the lieutenant's test and scored fairly well. I was in the top twelve, but there were few lieutenant vacancies and I had to wait my turn. About six months later, I was notified to report to the chief's conference room, known as the Round Table (because it really was round) for a promotional interview. This was new to me. I didn't have to be interviewed for promotion to sergeant, but since then this new procedure had been instituted. I waited in the hall with other applicants, and we nervously joked about how the interviewee's chair would be wet with sweat. The door to the room opened, and the applicant who interviewed before us came out looking pale and stricken.

"Gary Dias?" came the soft call from within.

I entered the room. The table was encircled with assistant chiefs, and at the head of the table sat Deputy Chief Warren Ferreira.

"Gary, sit down," he said, and pointed to the only empty chair in the room.

It was wet.

When I sat down, I realized I could hear my heart pounding. I remember thinking, "Don't faint, don't faint, don't faint."

The interview started with one assistant chief (A/C) asking me why I wanted to be promoted. What an asinine question.

"Sir, I believe that I can be an asset to this department in any lieutenant's assignment." I wonder how many times he heard that same response that day? Another A/C asked the second question.

"Your record shows that you were sick twice last year. What's that all about?"

I think my mouth was hanging open, because I thought I was hearing him criticize me for being sick for two days.

"I think I had the flu."

"You think?"

"Ah . . . yes, it was the flu."

He shot me an *I don't believe you* look.

It was Deputy Chief Ferreira's turn.

"We have an opening in Communications Division. Are you able to work with women?" Communications Division, a.k.a. Dispatch, was probably 85 percent women, and in retrospect, I understand the question. Some police officers have a difficult time working with civilians, and an even more difficult time when the civilians are women.

I don't understand why I said what I did, but it flowed from my mouth.

"I've been married ten years."

Ferreira and most of the others burst into laughter. I was panicked. Did they think I was trying to be funny? Did they think I was being sarcastic? Did I just seal my fate?

I was excused. The interviewee's chair was wetter than before. I stumbled away, looking pale and stricken.

About two weeks later, Inspector Doane walked into my office and sat down. He smiled and paused and nodded his head.

"Congratulations, Lieutenant. You're on your way to Communications Division."

I was very happy at this news. The inspector shook my hand, smiled broadly again and got up. He stopped at my door and turned back to me with a somber face.

"But you know, Dias, you gotta learn not to be such a bad ass."

29
Dispatch

My new assignment was as the executive relief lieutenant for the Communications Division, a.k.a. Dispatch. The division was laid out in an "L" shape, with the radio consoles and call takers along the long arm of the unit, and the administrative offices and squad room in the shorter section.

Most of my duties were administrative: preparing for IA inspections, answering complaints against the dispatchers, and performing any other functions handed down by the captain. Occasionally, I relieved the watch lieutenants when they took vacation or other leave. I really enjoyed that aspect of the job because it allowed me to feel closer to the patrol action.

The Communications Division assignment was similar to being a desk sergeant. It was a first step for new lieutenants, who didn't stay there long, usually until the next batch of lieutenants came along. We all knew our stint there was probably going to be short, so we made the most of our stay.

Learning to run a radio as a dispatcher was one of the most interesting activities. As officers, we were concerned about listening for our call numbers. Dispatchers were concerned about all the officers on their frequency, perhaps as many as twenty to twenty-five, not to mention the other units in the department who tested on their frequency. I remain amazed at the skill some of those dispatchers had in handling all the calls and activities happening on their radios. Like all other divisions, however, Dispatch was understaffed. We had too many vacancies, and it was difficult for the dispatchers to get special time off, but most never complained, adding to my admiration of them.

The way dispatch worked in my time there was simple. A call

Communications Division. The call takers forward the information down the track to the radio dispatchers, who assign officers to cases.

came in to one of the call takers, who wrote down the complaint on a card. The card was sent on a moving track to the respective dispatcher, who sent the proper officer. The dispatcher logged information on the card, such as which officer was sent, the time of the call, the times an officer was sent and arrived at the scene, and the time the officer was back from the case. The card was then sent to the "back room," where t was entered into the computer and a report number was issued. Not a difficult process, unless it got busy and we were short-handed.

Today, everything is computerized. A call comes in to a call taker, who inputs the information into a computer. Simultaneously, a dispatcher receives the information on his or her computer screen. The dispatcher dispatches an officer and inputs the times sent, arrived, and back. The times are automatically logged into the Report Management System (RMS), and the computer program automatically assigns the case a report number. When the officers type their reports into the computer, the information is instantly tied to the initial information inputted by the dispatcher and stored in the Records Division computerized report files.

My eight months in the Communications Division were pretty routine, except for a couple of episodes with big, bad-luck Irish Lieutenant Jack. Jack was physically domineering. He was tall and very large and could pass for the old-time Irish cop from turn-of-the-century New York or Chicago that you see in movies. Shortly after Jack and I were promoted, Honolulu Mayor Frank Fasi won his comeback re-election bid against Eileen Anderson. One of the first things he did was have the department install a direct telephone line from the dispatch lieutenant's desk to his home. We didn't have to dial. We just picked up the receiver and it rang on the other end. Jack was on his two days off when the telephone was installed, and when he came back I heard his loud voice bellow out over the radio consoles, in his distinctive Irish accent.

"What's with this phone, here?"

"That's a direct line to Mayor Fasi's house," answered a diminutive voice from the call taker tracks.

"Oh, yeah, sure," Jack retorted, moving on to another issue. I remember thinking I would explain the telephone when I had a minute. But as fate would have it, the phone rang before anyone could fill Jack in as to why it was hanging there on the wall. The one-sided conversation went something like this.

"Hello!" bellowed Jack in his normal loud voice.

"Oh, yeah, sure, and I'm Joyce Fasi. We're busy over here; who the hell is this?"

"Okay, *Mayor Fasi*, if you insist. Go run the city, we're busy over here."

The whole room was quiet. Even the phones were quiet. Everyone was gaping at Lieutenant Jack in disbelief. A few minutes later, our division commander was called to the chief's office. When he returned, he called Jack to his office and I took a break outside.

A few weeks later, I was briefed in the morning that another incident with Lieutenant Jack occurred the night before. It seems that Jack was on duty when Chief Gibb's wife called. She told him that the chief was on the Big Island at a conference and she needed to let him know that there was a family emergency. She asked Lieutenant Jack to contact the Big island police and pass the message on to the chief. It seems that Lieutenant Jack forgot. The next morning, the chief called the division commander to his office. When he returned, all the supervisors were called together and informed that when a high-ranking officer or dignitary called, we were to respond to that request immediately. He further instructed us that the chief wanted someone at the lieutenant's console at all times to take important calls. Did we all understand? Yes.

A few days later, as we subsequently learned, the chief called the lieutenant's console for some reason. The phone rang off the hook. Seems that Lieutenant Jack walked outside for something and forgot to put a dispatcher at the console. The chief, particularly exasperated from all these telephone-call incidents, called the division commander again. About thirty seconds before his telephone rang, the division commander notified the secretary that he was walking out to get a candy bar. The secretary got up and went to the bathroom, and I walked into the dispatch console room on business. When I returned to my desk, the division commander had just returned, sat down at his desk, and put his feet up as he opened his candy bar and took a bite. At about the time he bit into the chocolate, the chief burst into the division. He looked at the dispatch major and said, "Come see me in my office, now."

I never saw ears as red as our major's were when he returned. And I do believe that the telephone at the lieutenant's console never rang more than once ever again.

30
Back to CID

My time assigned to the Communications Division gave me an appreciation of the work done there, but my first love was fieldwork, so I requested a transfer when a field assignment became available. (Little did I realize then that I would never again be reassigned to a patrol division.) Word came that I was being assigned back to CID as the lieutenant in charge of my old Burglary/Theft Detail. It wasn't patrol, but it was close enough, and I jumped at the opportunity to go back. It didn't take long for me to realize that the job was different. I wasn't investigating burglaries or thefts; I was managing a detail. I was reading and correcting reports. I was reviewing and assigning cases. I was submitting monthly statistical reports. I had to come to grips with it: I was now administration.

One of our duties was to prepare statistical reports for the department to send to the FBI. There are two major criminal data collection methods: the Uniform Crime Report (UCR), maintained by the FBI, and the National Crime Victimization Survey, maintained by the Department of Justice. Both methodologies gather and report data, but in very different ways. The FBI collects data from law enforcement agencies across the nation. The NCVS conducts surveys of crime victims. There are problems with both methods.

The UCR depends on data provided by police agencies. It assumes that each agency reports data in the same way. And there's the problem. Different agencies do not always report data in the same way. Why? One answer is that different agencies have different requirements or quotas placed on their detectives. Police agencies do not like to report that their burglary arrests and case closings are below the national average. So pressure is put on individual detectives to come up with the statistics to meet, at the least, minimum standards. Another answer to why agencies differ in reporting standards involves the manipulation of the data. One old detective once said to me, "Tell me the closing percentage you want, and I'll give it to you every time." That's possible only if you manipulate data. For example, assume a Burg/Theft Detail had one hundred cases to solve last month. Out of these cases, only thirty of them had any solvability factors. Those thirty cases were assigned to detectives to investigate. The remaining seventy were filed pending developments. Of the thirty assigned cases, detectives solved fifteen of them. An unscrupulous commander would then report that his detectives solved 50 percent of their cases. That commander is not actually lying. He's just not reporting the true data, which should show a closing rate of only 15 percent, well below the national average (at that time) of 18 to 20 percent burglary closings.

There are fifteen thousand separate law-enforcement agencies across the country, ranging from small-town sheriffs' departments to police agencies in large metropolitan cities and many statewide forces, such as the New York State Police. Each agency receives instructions from the FBI on how to close cases and on what can be reported to the UCR, for example, but inherent differences in the many agencies prevent the data from being accurate.

The National Crime Victimization Survey has different problems. It is based on interviews with crime victims, and crime victims may not all classify cases the same way. For example, a question may be, "Were you robbed last year?" A person who came home from work and found that his home was burglarized may say, "We were robbed!" A misunderstanding of case classification occurs, and wrong data is given. In addition, some people may be too embarrassed to admit they were victims of crimes. Some women who are rape victims never report the crime out of embarrassment. Also, not all crimes are reported via the NCVS. How does one answer, "Were you a victim of homicide last year?" or "Were you a victim of prostitution last year?"

Working the Burg/Theft Detail as a lieutenant was not as exciting as it initially seemed. Then one day, the CID captain in charge of violent crime investigation asked me if I would be interested in being the lieutenant in charge of the Robbery Detail. At times like these, when you think that Christmas came early, you try not to let on that you're about to pop with excitement. Of course, I would love to be the lieutenant of the Robbery Detail.

And with that came a desk in the safe. The department occupied the old Sears building at 1455 S. Beretania Street, and the Criminal Investigation Division was located in the dungeon—I mean, basement. Sears had an old safe there that was left intact when the department took over the building. It became my office, complete with a large door with a combination dial. It was just another windowless office, except the walls were made of solid reinforced concrete and the door was eight inches of steel. It was quieter than other offices along the long CID hall.

The old police headquarters at 1455 S. Beretania Street

The Robbery Detail handled all types of robberies, including bank robberies. Robbing a bank is a federal offense that is normally handled by the FBI. In Honolulu during the early eighties, the FBI deferred the investigation to HPD detectives. The thought process behind this was that the local detectives had a better relationship with criminals who commit robberies and would have an easier time obtaining information than a group of mainland agents from various cultures on the mainland. The FBI would, however, often prosecute in federal court using our investigation as their basis of proof.

Bank robbery investigation involved many aspects: latent fingerprints, video recordings, witnesses, and exploding dye packs, to name a few. A dye pack is made to resemble a wad of money. It is actually an exploding paper and cardboard pack with a dye-and-tear-gas canister that we hope will stain the suspect and temporarily incapacitate him. An electronic device is placed near the door, and when the suspect leaves the bank, the device activates the dye pack, which will usually explode within thirty seconds. As the pack explodes and releases the gas and dye, it gets very hot. In one notable case, a man robbed a downtown bank. As he left the bank, he stuffed the package of money down the front of his pants. Oh yes. A few seconds after he left the bank, the pack exploded. In his pants. His pants caught fire. His groin caught fire. Responding officers received reports of a man naked from the waist down, with fluorescent orange legs, groin, and waist. He was running down the street, looking as if he was trying to put out a fire in his pubic area. He was soon apprehended.

Sometimes, crooks show just how stupid they are. One walked into the bank, tore a deposit ticket from his personal checkbook, wrote a robbery demand note on the back, and handed it to a teller. Another robbed his aunt, who was a teller at a particular bank. Asked later why he picked someone he knew, he said he did not feel intimidated by her. Quick-thinking tellers have insisted that robbers sign receipts for the money or provide ID. Sometimes they do.

At other times a little investigating will lead us to the robber's door. A guy robbed a teller with a demand note that read, "Give me the money and no one will get hurt." The paper he used came from a notepad and had indentations on it. Upon closer scrutiny, the indentations revealed that he recently put an ad in the newspaper to sell his car and gave his telephone number. Hello? Anyone home? But think about it. Robbing a bank is just about the only crime during which you are guaranteed to be photographed.

One of the things the robbery detail did very well was handling a lineup. In-station lineups took place in the basement of the main headquarters, next to the patrol squad room. Field lineups, on the other hand, took place in the community, usually where the suspect was apprehended. In a field lineup, or show-up as it was also known, the suspect was allowed to stand near the apprehending police officers while the victim or witness was driven by. The officer with the victim or witness simply said, "Do you recognize anyone?"

The in-station lineup required officers to find five or six people who looked like the suspect in terms of race, age, height, weight, and other physical characteristics. It was always preferable to find people from the community willing to participate. Detectives went out and found people who looked like the suspect and offered them twenty-five dollars for their participation. We never suffered for willing participants. From time to time, however, we used police officers who looked like the suspect. In these cases, the officers participated on duty or on overtime, but they did not receive the participant stipend. Using officers was an infrequent practice because the officers usually looked cleaner and smarter than the crook. And they looked—and talked and walked—like police officers. If the other participants didn't look enough like the suspect, there was a risk that we could lose the lineup evidence in a defense motion or appeal. To avoid that, we looked for normal people. Police officers, because of the higher standards placed on them, don't look normal. And when they're standing in a lineup, they tend to stand tall and sneer at the suspect, who's the only guy hunched over and sulking.

The lineup room was like a minitheater with rows of seats. At the back of the room was a two-way mirror the witness could look through to view the lineup without being seen by the suspect.

The suspect and five or six look-alikes stood at the front of the room on a stage. Each of them had a large number hanging on his chest. The suspect selected the position he wished to stand in, and who he wanted standing next to him. If the suspect had an attorney, the attorney could provide input. The one thing the suspect could not do was refuse to participate in the lineup. Those who refused to obtain an attorney were given a public defender, who always advised the suspect to participate in the lineup.

After the suspect and look-alikes were situated, the witnesses were brought in and allowed to look at the group. Each lineup participant was instructed to come down from the stage and approach the mirror. While standing in front of the mirror, he was instructed to turn to the right four times, making a complete turn. If words were spoken in the robbery, he was asked to speak the words used by the perpetrator and then return to the stage. The witnesses were then taken to separate locations and interviewed. At no time did the detective ask if the witness saw the suspect. That is a leading question, indicating that a suspect is in the room. The witnesses were simply asked if they recognized anyone. A color photograph was taken of the lineup showing all the participants exactly as they looked to the witnesses.

One incident is a reminder that most crooks have the intelligence of a gingerroot. When one bank robber got to the mirror during his lineup, he was asked to say aloud, "Give me the money and no one will get hurt." The suspect looked around as if he were searching for the detective and said, "But that's not what I said. I said, give me the money and I won't hurt you." Most times it's not that easy.

A field lineup sometimes has the same requirements. Howard, one of CID's theft detectives, was sent to Mānoa, where two teen-age boys were arrested for burglarizing a house. Both boys were about fourteen years old, part-Polynesian, and darkly tanned. Howard, nearing retirement, was not as enthusiastic as many a younger detective was, but realized he needed to conduct a field lineup because there were several neighbors who witnessed the boys break into the house. It would have been fine if Howard had simply driven the neighbors past the boys and let the neighbors ID them, but he thought he needed to conduct a lineup as done by the Robbery Detail. A quick check around the neighborhood produced no similar suspects, so he lined up the two boys and used four of the police officers as his other participants.

Howard quickly realized he had some problems. The boys were dressed in shorts and colored T-shirts. The officers had on their long blue uniform pants and similar white undershirts. The boys were both about five feet four inches tall. Each of the officers was almost six feet tall. Howard thought about it for a minute, then found the solution.

"Everyone stand behind that small rock wall. Good. Now, everyone take off your shirt. Good. Now, police officers, kneel down." And he photographed the lineup with his Polaroid Instamatic.

The neighbors identified the boys. Howard was happy—until his lineup was thrown out of court. He couldn't understand why. They were all bareback, so the clothing differences didn't come into play. They were all the same height, so that didn't matter. He showed us the color photo. The part-Polynesian boys were dark skinned; the police officers were pale. The officers were at least ten years older than the boys. A totally clueless person could pick out the two suspects. None of this quite clicked with Howard. Luckily though, both boys confessed and were convicted in spite of the lineup from hell.

31
Hostage Negotiations

During my tenure as the Robbery Detail lieutenant, I was also given the responsibility to command the department's Hostage Negotiation Team. I joked with my boss that I couldn't understand why because I didn't have the patience for anything. He smiled and said, "I don't want *you* to negotiate with anyone. I want you to be in charge of the team. Pick good people to negotiate." So with my orders in hand, I did just that.

Prior to the decision to create a formal negotiation team, whenever the department needed a negotiator, certain detectives were always used—partly because of their experience, partly because of their patience. But now we needed a formal team. The establishment of the team under the authority of the Criminal Investigation Division seemed appropriate. Some people favor placing the negotiating team under the authority of the Specialized Services Division, with the Specialized Weapons and Tactics (SWAT) Team. But I believe it is better to separate the two, because of the potential for conflict when one team is responsible for using force to end a dangerous hostage incident, while the other is responsible for ending it peacefully.

A primary fact about hostage negotiations is that they are a form of communication. An actual negotiation is a test of the negotiator's skills, knowledge, and patience. The FBI has placed hostage incidents into four classifications: 1) the prison hostage incident, 2) the terrorist hostage incident 3) a criminal incident in which a hostage has been taken, and 4) an incident in which the hostage taker is mentally disturbed. In all these incidents, however, the hostage negotiator depends on his or her ability to communicate with the hostage taker.

In all cases, the negotiator must be able to get the hostage taker to talk. It is through this conversation that information is obtained, specific knowledge is learned, and a course of action decided. The better the rapport between the negotiator and the hostage taker, the longer the discussions and conversations will last. And time is beneficial to the police. Case studies have shown that most hostage incidents end peacefully with the passage of time and continuing discussions between the negotiator and hostage taker.

Most studies identify several goals in hostage incidents. The first goal is for the negotiator to obtain information from the hostage taker regarding why the incident occurred. This helps the SWAT team or other officers to better plan and helps the negotiator to better speak to the hostage taker. In addition to getting information about the hostage taker's motivation, the negotiator tries to quickly learn his intent.

The second goal is similar to the first in that the negotiator now directs the discussions to learn as much as possible about the hostage taker. What are his demands? What does he expect to happen by taking a hostage?

The third goal is that the negotiator successfully imparts a sincere interest in the hostage taker's needs, problems, worries, and demands. Sometimes, he simply needs to be heard. The relationship between the hostage taker and the negotiator is a tenuous one. The negotiator must never, ever lie to the hostage taker. If the hostage taker suspects that the negotiator has lied, the relationship is usually over and becomes very difficult to reestablish. For example, if a hostage taker demands a getaway car, the negotiator never wants to say one is on the way. It is always better to change the direction of the discussion in an effort to resolve the issue. It may even be better to let the hostage taker know that the police will not allow him to drive away.

Last, it is the ultimate goal of the police in hostage negotiations to end the incident peacefully, without any bloodshed. All efforts must be taken to preserve the safety of all, including the hostage taker.

The negotiator must keep the conversation going. He must avoid questions the hostage taker can answer with a simple yes or no. It's important to keep the hostage taker thinking—and talking—about the situation.

Negotiators and police administrators should comply with simple demands. Food, for example, should always be allowed. Providing food is easy and shows the hostage taker that the negotiator is credible and that the police want to end the incident peacefully. It is important to the negotiator's continued credibility with the hostage taker never to appear to be the person who is able to meet demands. The hostage taker should be told that all demands and requests must be approved by higher authorities back at headquarters. The negotiator, however, should never say no to a hostage taker's demands. He should take a neutral stance and defer all demands to a higher authority.

From time to time, in media reports of hostage incidents, the hostage taker's relatives speak out angrily about the police. "If they would have just let me speak to him, it would be over by now." The police should never let anyone besides the negotiator speak to the hostage taker. We simply do not know the relationship between the hostage taker and the person who wants to speak to him. The relationship could be the driving force for the hostage taker to harm a hostage or commit suicide. The ultimate goal of the negotiations is to end the incident without bloodshed. Occasionally, a police department allows a relative to speak to the hostage taker. That is a bad precedent. Many times, such decisions are made by administrators who are miles away and not educated in the field of hostage negotiations.

We had an incident in Pālolo in which a man had a bad fight with his wife and beat her. The man greeted arriving officers saying he would kill his wife and kids if the officers tried to interfere. The initial officers surrounded his residence and called for SWAT backup and negotiators. People sometimes say, why don't the police just go away? We can't. We simply can't. If we leave, the hostage taker may

SWAT training in full gear at Ke Kula Mākaʻi

feel more courageous and decide to take more hostages at a fast food restaurant or a bank. The police simply can't leave.

We arrived on the scene and established a negotiating command post near the SWAT command truck. Soon, a negotiator was speaking to the hostage taker. It was early afternoon. The discussions continued throughout the night and into the early morning hours. Finally, the hostage taker told the negotiator, "I'm tired. I want to go to sleep." The negotiator answered with a normal response: "Okay, I'll talk to you in the morning." About five minutes later a woman and her two sleepy children came out of the house and told officers that her husband was sleeping in the bedroom. Officers quietly entered and arrested him. No one was hurt. Time was once again the best weapon the police had.

The best way police negotiators can hone their skills is to practice, practice, practice. We train for scenarios that include all possible types of incidents. Training allows officers to understand SWAT methods, know their equipment, and develop confidence. We often trained with the SWAT team and the military. The armed services had interested and willing personnel and enabled their military police and administrative officers to obtain the same much-needed training.

We once trained with the Navy SEALS. It was a two-day weekend exercise with the scenario that terrorists had taken people in a house hostage. The first scenario that weekend ended an hour after it started. The HPD SWAT command truck was parked over a manhole, and shortly afterward a Navy SEAL "terrorist" crawled out of the sewer and tossed a dummy hand grenade into the truck. HPD SWAT 0, Navy SEALS 1. We learned never to underestimate the people we are dealing with.

I commanded the Hostage Negotiation Team for about eight years and responded to many incidents with them and the Specialized Services Division's SWAT Team. From my perspective, the negotiators and the SSD men and women tackle a most physically and mentally challenging job and conduct themselves in a most professional manner. I will always remain proud to have worked with them.

32
Homicide

During the late seventies, when I served as the Sector Seven sergeant, I responded to a report of a woman's body being found in her apartment near Kāheka Street. I arrived and met with the first officer, who looked somber. He pointed inside and said, "We have a homicide." I slowly entered the apartment, looking around the floor so I didn't step on anything I'd be better off not stepping on. In the wide opening between the bedroom and living room, a woman in her late twenties or early thirties was lying on the floor on her stomach. Her legs were bent at the knees at a ninety-degree angle, and a long telephone cord was wrapped around her ankles. The cord went from her ankles to her head, where it was tightly wrapped around her neck, creating a deep furrow in her skin. Her face was splotchy purple and her eyes were open, staring toward the door. I touched her cheek. It was hard and cold. I walked outside and pulled my portable radio from its pouch.

"One-six-nine. Notify Homicide."

The first two people to arrive from the Homicide Detail were the lieutenant and one detective. I briefed them and stood in the outdoor corridor of the apartment as both of them walked into the room. Both were smoking. One squatted next to the woman's body; the other bent over her. Cigarette ashes fell onto her hair. One of them swatted her head to keep the ashes from burning her hair.

On the table in the living room was a checkbook. One of the investigators thumbed through the checkbook as the other sat on the couch, put his cigarette out in an ashtray that was already half full of cigarettes, and used the telephone—the same telephone whose long cord was used to strangle the woman. As he spoke to someone at CID, he also thumbed through papers on the table.

It was a scene that burned into my memory. It was obscene. It was disrespectful to the murdered woman. It pitifully lacked any degree of professiona ism. Yet it was typical of the follow-up investigative process at the time. Back then, major crime investigation involved three steps:

First, we documented the crime scene by taking pictures and making a diagram. Second, we collected all the physical evidence *we could see*. And third, we interviewed everyone who knew the victim; someone in that group was the killer. We hoped; most homicide victims knew their killer. There was little concern about trace evidence at this time in the department because courts didn't place a high value on such evidence or even the processing of such evidence. What counted the most was documentation of the scene so that it could be portrayed accurately to the court; statements; and confessions. But something happened to Hawai'i trials over the years. We caught up with mary mainland jurisdictions and court requirements, and in less than a decade, investigative requirements changed. Confessions were still important, but they no longer held the ultimate position in the hierarchy of an investigation.

In 1986, the man who then served as homicide lieutenant retired. Everyone in CID placed their bets on two lieutenants to succeed him. Both had served as homicide detectives some years earlier, and both had some good characteristics and some not-so-good characteristics. Weeks passed and rumors flew. Some administrators liked Lieutenant X, some liked Lieutenant Y. What we were beginning to hear was that the bad points of these two good men were becoming the key issues for administrators. Threats were made, or so we heard. If Lieutenant X is selected, you must add these other people to the detail to keep him in check. If Lieutenant Y is selected, you'll need a new major, because the current major will not be able to control him, and on and on.

One day, my captain walked into my office and didn't mince words.

"They can't decide on who they want as the homicide lieutenant, and we've been asked to look for an alternate candidate. Would you like to be considered?"

Oh, hell, yes, you damn fool, you don't even have to ask, you know any one of us would jump at the chance, I thought.

"Well, I've never considered it before you mentioned it, but yeah, okay, sure," I said.

And that's how I came to be the homicide lieutenant. I was someone's third choice, a compromise candidate. I wasn't politically connected to anyone, I didn't belong to anyone's clique, I didn't regularly go drinking with anyone. How the hell did I get selected? I think administrators felt I could be controlled. I was a neutral personality to most. But I was also someone they knew from my various assignments in the department. And because I had only fifteen years in the department, my salary was in a medium range. This was an important consideration, because the homicide lieutenant was on call twenty-four hours a day, all year long. And for this imposition, he got twenty-five percent more pay. Twenty-five percent of my salary was much less than twenty-five percent of the salary of either Lieutenant X or Lieutenant Y. I also had six years of investigative experience under my belt, and I had been a supervisor for ten years.

Third choice or not, I had just been assigned to one of the most prestigious lieutenant positions in the department. In my mind, it was one of the most important positions I ever held. I remembered the image of that murdered young woman lying on her stomach with a telephone cord wrapped tightly around her neck and an investigator swatting her head to keep his cigarette ash from burning her hair. And from the start, I promised myself that when I investigated a homicide, respect for the victim would be a part of the investigation, because someone had lost a son or a daughter, a sister or a brother. Fulfilling that vow was easy, because during the eight years since that young woman had been murdered, the level of professionalism of the detail had become extremely high, and I was taking over from a homicide lieutenant who devoted himself to having his men conduct the best homicide investigations possible.

Early on in my stint with the homicide detail, I was sent to homicide seminars in Albany, New York, and at the FBI Academy in Quantico, Virginia. There I learned that the trend in homicide investigations was to pay great attention to trace evidence. Confessions did not hold the same importance they once did. Courts placed an ever increasing importance on physical evidence, and much of that evidence is minute or unseen.

Trace evidence is a generic term for small, often microscopic evidence. It's based on a theory developed by a French scientist, Edmund Locard, which says that when two objects come into contact with each other, each object leaves evidence of its presence on the other and takes away evidence of the other object. Locard's Theory has been shown time and again to be true. Therefore, when a police officer or detective says there is no evidence at a crime scene, he's wrong. He just hasn't looked hard enough. And that's the primary job of a crime-scene investigation. The evidence is there; we just have to find it.

The homicide seminars also taught me that other jurisdictions devote needed resources, in terms of staffing, equipment, and funding, to homicide investigations. In Honolulu at that time, we were having a funding crunch, and we were frequently told that very little money was available to spend on overtime. One year, a list was prepared identifying areas that would receive special funding because the proper investigation of those offenses was important to the community. The top money went to white collar crime. Homicide didn't even make the list. The murder of a human being has become so commonplace that it's considered a normal crime that should be investigated with funds allotted within the budget. Television and movies have a lot to do with creating the image that killing a human being is a clean, emotionless, event that the cops solve in under an hour. Did you ever notice that most of the murders committed on *NYPD Blue* are solved in the interview room?

Most successful homicide investigations are solved in the first seventy-two hours. The homicide team needs to conduct follow-up interviews as soon as possible after the murder occurs, while emotions are still high and while suspects are still forming their lies and alibis. And while one group of detectives is conducting interviews, another is completing the crime scene investigation. This usually involves paying overtime to get the job done right and in a timely manner. (Years later at The Queen's Medical Center, I would learn the concept of *kinaole* from the late author and Hawaiian historian George Kanahele. *Kinaole*, he taught, was a philosophy of old Hawai'i that maintained that no matter your job—canoe builder, woodworker, fisherman, taro grower—you conducted yourself in such a way that you did the right thing, for the right person, at the right time, at the right location, for the right reasons—the first time. In other words, your effort was expected to be the best the first time. Every time.)

I was questioned time and again by administrators who didn't understand the value of trace evidence: "Why do you people take so long to process a crime scene?" When those old-time administrators had conducted murder investigations thirty years earlier, they were, in their words, "in and out of that crime scene in an hour." That may have been fine for the standard of proof accepted by courts in the fifties and sixties. But today, defense attorneys educated in forensic science and investigative techniques demand that police provide better proof. It was extraordinarily frustrating to have administrators insist that we investigate a homicide to a lesser degree of completion or that we purposely strive for something less than perfection.

In 1989, Police Officer David Ronk was murdered by Clyde Pinero while trying to serve a Temporary Restraining Order (TRO) on him. He and fellow officers went to a Wai'anae address where Pinero had previously threatened his wife. His wife had obtained a TRO, and the officers were going to serve it. When Pinero answered the door, he saw the officers and ran. Ronk gave chase. Another officer went around the back. Ronk caught up to Pinero in the bedroom and applied a judo choke hold from behind. Pinero reached back, grabbed Ronk's service revolver from his holster, brought it up over his head, and shot Ronk. The bullet struck Ronk on the shoulder and ricocheted into his heart. He died later at the hospital. The suspect threw the gun on the bed and was arrested by other officers who rushed into the house.

Homicide responded to the scene, along with many, many administrators. When a police officer is killed, administrators all rush to the scene, forgetting the rules of crime-scene preservation. In Ronk's case, when HPD administrators arrived, I briefed them on the status of the case. I informed them that we were preparing a search warrant for the house. They got angry and told me we didn't need a search warrant. I described the conditions—that it was the home of the suspect and we would need a search warrant to protect the evidence. I was told that if I wouldn't follow their instructions, they would find a homicide lieutenant who would. After all, one said, this was a crime scene, and the police had the right to search a crime scene. He apparently gave no thought to the Fourth Amendment.

I was offended that administrators would micromanage a homicide case—and the murder of a police officer at that. I was offended that this administrator, who was obviously not aware of the legal requirements of a search of a suspect's home, would possibly jeopardize the future conviction of the suspect. I called the prosecutor's office and relayed the situation. Based on the visible evidence, the gun on the bed, and the fact that the suspect was the only other person with Ronk when he was shot, the prosecutor thought we had a strong case, in spite of not being able to search the house thoroughly. He did advise that anything else recovered by searching the suspect's house would probably be lost in court as a result of the Exclusionary Rule, which states that any evidence recovered in an unreasonable search and seizure is excluded from being presented as evidence at a trial.

I could not understand why, at that crime scene, police administrators wanted the investigation rushed. I was told later, but could not corroborate it, that they wanted to tell the media that HPD charged the suspect the same day as the killing. I hope that was a false rumor. We should never jeopardize the investigation of a murder in order to look good. A crime-scene investigation must be thorough. It is from the crime scene that we obtain evidence to identify the suspect. Perhaps more important, it is where we establish the *corpus delicti*, the body of the crime, or the elements that make up the criminal offense.

So what is a crime scene? "Where the crime happened," you might answer. That's only partially true. Too often, police officers forget that there is another aspect to the definition. The complete definition is "that physical location where a crime occurred, to include avenues of approach to the scene and escape from the scene by the suspect." If we don't consider how and where the suspect approached the crime scene or how and where he or she fled, we may stand to lose valuable evidence. In cases of homicide or other major cases such as rape, the victim's body and clothing, as well as the suspect's body and clothing, should be considered crime scenes in and of themselves. In cases where there has been physical interaction or assault between victim and suspect, their bodies and clothing may yield a great deal of evidence that could place the two of them together.

Understanding what a crime scene is leads to understanding what *crime-scene preservation* is. Crime-scene preservation has two-parts: First, the crime scene should be kept in the same condition the perpetrator left it in. This helps investigators understand the dynamics of the offense and helps them reconstruct the crime. A very important step in any crime-scene investigation is for the investigator to stand just outside the crime scene and look at the condition of the scene. I didn't coin the phrase, but I use it: *Let the crime scene talk to you*. Shakespeare said it most eloquently in *Hamlet*: "For murder, though it have no tongue, will speak." Our job as investigators is to let the crime scene speak to us and be sure to listen to what it's saying. Forensics? Trace evidence? Arson? Latent fingerprints? Ballistics? Consultation with an entomologist who can provide valuable insights through the study of the insects at the crime scene?

The second part of crime-scene preservation is to prevent the adding to or taking away from the crime scene of any items that may be evidence. Why would police officers in their right minds add to or take away evidence from a crime scene? Normally, they don't. But officers—especially administrators—have a propensity to walk all over crime scenes and touch things. When we walk through a crime scene, we track in trace items via the soles of our shoes. We also shed. Everything sheds. But people shed hair and skin and fibers from their clothing. (In my case, I shed hair at an alarming rate.) We deposit items that can be construed as evidence in a crime scene simply by walking through it. And while we're doing that, we're picking up actual evidence, perhaps on the soles of our shoes, and taking it away from the scene.

In 1987, Police Officer Troy Barboza was murdered as he lay on his living room couch. The murderer was Tony Williams, a drug dealer and gang member from Los Angeles. Barboza was going to testify against Williams in a drug case. When homicide detectives arrived, we found administrators from many different divisions walking around the crime scene. Barboza still lay on the couch, but administrators were looking around the living room, picking things up, using the telephone, drinking coffee, and smoking cigarettes.

For God's sake, I thought, *this is the murder scene of one of our own and you're all walking about it as if it were some kind of grotesque gallery at a circus sideshow.* When they finally left us to our work, we processed the scene. Right at the window where Williams fired the weapon, we found a glistening latent fingerprint. Latent fingerprints are made when we touch objects with our fingers, which are oily from perspiration. When we found that seemingly fresh latent print, we did not know who the suspect was, so we were ecstatic at finding such a valuable piece of evidence. Months later, when we identified Barboza's killer, we ran a comparison between Williams' fingerprints and the latent print we found. They didn't match. This created a big problem. We had good leads on the killer, but right at the spot where the killer fired his weapon, the fresh fingerprint wasn't his. Think of the defense attorney arguing that we had the wrong man. We believed the latent was left by a police administrator. We wanted to get the prints of our administrators to compare and eliminate the latent, but they all refused to cooperate. (We didn't have all their fingerprints already on file because a fire destroyed a number of police records some years prior. Or so we were told.) Why did they refuse to cooperate? Because it would have been embarrassing for them to have left latent fingerprints at the murder scene of a fellow police officer.

So we know that we need to preserve the evidence at a crime scene. What is *evidence,* then? That question has an easy answer, too. But it has a qualification. Evidence is *anything* that can be presented at a trial that proves guilt or innocence, *providing* it can be presented legally. There are many types and forms of evidence.

Real, or physical evidence is anything that has existence, breadth, width, and depth. Testimonial evidence consists of statements and confessions. Both real and testimonial evidence can be either direct evidence or circumstantial evidence. Direct evidence is exactly what it states: evidence that directly proves a fact. For example, if a bullet taken from the body of a dead man exactly matches a bullet recovered from a test fire of a suspect's weapon, that proves that the bullet in the body came from that particular gun. It does not prove who fired the gun. Circumstantial evidence requires interpretation. Here is where it becomes a little more difficult. A prosecutor must argue his or her points to get the judge or jury to interpret the evidence his or her way. Defense attorneys will argue to have them interpret it their way.

The traditional methods of investigating a crime scene still exist and are also important at a crime scene. Major processes are done at crime scenes: searches, diagrams, and photos.

What we had going for us in 1986 when we conducted homicide investigations was a dedicated group of evidence specialists. These men and women sought to improve the ways we locate and collect evidence. Their work was extraordinary. Each of the evidence specialists was skilled in the traditional tasks of searches, diagrams, and crime-scene photography. When they weren't working cases, many of them were working on new ways to identify and process items to gather evidence. One such specialist is Evidence Specialist Clarence Frasier. Clarence helped us teach recruits about crime-scene investigation and forensic science. At one class, I watched Clarence show a group of recruits how to obtain fingerprints from crumpled-up toilet paper. He also showed them how he developed a method of recovering latent fingerprints from human skin.

Some months later we responded to the murder of an elderly woman, who had been raped, sodomized, and strangled. One of the items of evidence was a clump of toilet paper soiled with feces. The suspect had apparently used the toilet paper to clean himself. It all came back.

"Clarence," I asked, "please recover that toilet paper and see if you can get fingerprints from it."

Clarence's look said, *You gotta be kidding.*

"Remember the recruit class when you showed us how you were able to lift fingerprints from toilet tissue?"

Without further question, Clarence recovered the paper. Back at the lab, he processed it. As a credit to his ever professional demeanor and efforts, he found latent fingerprints on it.

The problem with latent fingerprints is that we need to match the recovered latent prints to those identified in a database. While I was with the detail, we never solved that murder. But thanks to Clarence, in the files is latent fingerprint evidence waiting to be compared against a suspect's inked fingerprints.

We've come a long way in our homicide investigations from that day in the late seventies when an investigator slapped the head of a murdered woman so his cigarette ashes would not burn her hair. And we're a better department because of detectives who use up-to-date investigative techniques and who show respect and compassion for those whose murders they investigate.

33
Homicide: Part 2

One issue that came up when I was assigned to Homicide was my age. I had fifteen years with the department, but I was only thirty-five years old. In spite of the fact that I had more than ten years of experience as a supervisor and manager, some of the officers saw me as not only the new kid on the block, but also the young new kid on the block. And worse yet, the young new kid on the block with his own thoughts on the changing face of homicide investigations. One case in particular confirmed their opinion.

A young woman returned home from work one evening to her apartment in the Lanakila area. She parked her car and got out. As she walked from her car, her estranged boyfriend approached her and an argument began. He pulled a large knife from his pants and began stabbing her. Her screams drew the attention of the people who lived in the complex. The boyfriend stabbed her repeatedly, and she fell to the ground. He grabbed her car keys and drove off, leaving her to die on the parking lot asphalt.

Our team got to the scene and began the two-fold process of investigating the crime scene and interviewing witnesses. There was no question who the suspect was; the witnesses knew him by name. We completed our work at the scene and went to prepare a warrant for his arrest. The next morning, the victim's car was found parked nose-first up against the dead-end curb of Captain Cook Street near The Queen's Medical Center. Evidence specialists photographed the car, triangulated its position on the street, and dusted the exterior for latents. Our plan was to tow the car to the station so that the passenger compartment could be processed. Since the keys were in the ignition, one of my detectives offered to turn the car around. No, I told him, let's not disturb the inside, we need to process it for prints. We'll put the car on a dolly and tow it that way. My detective argued that the prints were not necessary because there were witnesses to the killing. I argued back that processing for prints was part of the complete investigation and I wanted the car to be processed thoroughly, in spite of the witnesses. He thought I was being too careful. Besides, he said, it would be easier for the tow truck to pick up the car from the front end. We argued for some time before I simply said, "Do it my way."

I was embarrassed that I had to argue with the detective in front of other people, so I walked away from the car, pretending to look for evidence on the side of the road. I was about fifty yards from the car when I heard it start up. The detective was sitting in the driver's seat, handling the same steering wheel and gearshift lever the killer had handled. He was turning the car around in spite of my instructions. I was upset at his failure to follow instructions, but even more disturbed by his failure to exhibit the three basic characteristics for investigations: organization, thoroughness, and caution.

Organization is a key concept because the last thing an investigation needs is a homicide detective who enters a crime scene and asks, "What the hell do I do now?" Thoroughness, too, is an absolute must. After we release a crime scene, we may not have a second chance to do something we should have done the first time. And caution is necessary because when we have multiple forensic tests to perform, we must make sure a particular test will not interfere with other tests.

A homicide investigation centers on the death of a person who was loved by other people. Homicide is the most heinous act one person can commit against another. It cannot be undone. Yet our society and our judicial system provide greater punishment, on the average, to people who commit white-collar crimes than to murderers.

Elizabeth was a beautiful young woman from England who was working at a bank in Hawai'i. Gunther was an unemployed man from Germany who took up with Elizabeth. Gunther, as described by

Elizabeth's friends, was a leech. He didn't work and had no income. He depended on Elizabeth for everything. Her friends told us she wanted to get rid of Gunther. Gunther didn't want to leave. Elizabeth was his ticket.

One night, Gunther ran to the apartment next to Elizabeth's screaming, "I killed her. Call the police, I killed Elizabeth." When officers arrived, Gunther attacked them and had to be restrained. In the bedroom, Elizabeth lay on the floor with a contact gunshot wound to her head.

A contact gunshot wound occurs when the muzzle of the weapon is pressed against the head or body when it is fired. This creates a unique type of injury. With the muzzle against skin, there is no escape for the gases that were created when the weapon was fired. When the bullet's primer ignites, it burns the gunpowder in the cartridge very quickly—so quickly, in fact, that it sounds like an explosion. When the powder burns, it creates expanding gases that separate the bullet from its shell casing and push the bullet out of the gun barrel. With the muzzle against skin, the expanding gases follow the bullet into the wound. When the muzzle is against skin and bone, some of the gas enters between the skin and bone, causing the skin to expand and pull away from the bone. When the skin expands beyond its ability to stretch, it tears in a star-shaped pattern. This injury pattern commonly occurs with contact gunshot wounds to the head. The bullet that killed Elizabeth entered her temple.

Later, at CID, Gunther was interviewed. We videotaped the interview. In the presence of detectives, Gunther found it difficult to speak. He sobbed loudly and uncontrollably. Saliva and mucus flowed from his mouth and nose as he hysterically mourned Elizabeth's death. We managed to get from him a statement that he and Elizabeth were playing sex games with the gun, but Gunther's hysterical condition made it impossible to continue. The detective offered to go get some coffee for Gunther. The moment the detective left the room, Gunther wiped his face and sat calmly, not realizing that he was still being videotaped. When he heard footsteps approaching the door, he began sobbing again, and the body fluids flowed once again. In his wallet was a card showing him to be an active member of the Screen Actor's Guild. We charged Gunther with murder in the second degree.

In court months later, Gunther cried and shook uncontrollably. We showed the jury the video. We were sure they would see through Gunther's façade. We were sure they would understand that his emotion was an act—an act he practiced and honed to gain their sympathy. They didn't. They bought his story, phony snot and all. The jury found him guilty of the lesser offense of manslaughter.

Two years later, I attended a conference in Waikīkī. When I reached the registration table, I was shocked to see Gunther sitting at the table registering the attendees. I really didn't give a hoot about the other people around me who may have been listening.

"When did they let you out of prison?" I asked in disgust. "Or did you escape?"

"I was released on parole about six months ago."

"You shot and killed your girlfriend and you spent less than three years in jail."

Gunther looked up at me and smiled. "Good behavior."

I leaned real close to his face and said quietly, "You murdered Elizabeth. I'm sure her friends would be real interested in knowing you're out of prison and where you work."

Gunther wasn't smiling anymore, and the officer I was with grabbed me by my shirt sleeve and pulled me away.

It's people like Gunther who manipulate the system. And the system, at least in this case, provided absolutely no justice for Elizabeth. But as difficult as it may be to accept court decisions they don't like, detectives must not use those decisions as a reason to do a poor job. We have no control over what a defense attorney does in court, or how a judge will rule on a specific issue, or how a jury votes. We have to continue to provide the best investigations possible. That's how we sleep at night—knowing that we did all we could do, knowing that we were organized, that we were thorough, and that we used caution in our investigations.

It really comes down to the dedication a homicide detective has to his or her work. When a detective loses that dedication, or never really had it to begin with, it's time for that detective to move on to other assignments.

Our investigations were aided by new tools and techniques. Luminol, for example. Luminol is a chemical used to test for the presence of blood, even after the site has been cleaned up. It became available to us in Hawai'i in the late eighties. We used this new technique at many scenes and to reinvestigate old cases—Diane Suzuki's murder, for example.

Early one morning, we were notified that a man's body had been found in a car at Ke'ehi Lagoon Park. Our first examination of his body showed that he had suffered a massive head wound that caused a great crack in his skull. He was sitting in the driver's seat, and the upper half of his body was leaning over onto the passenger seat. There was very little blood—an immediate indication that the man had been killed somewhere else. The head and brain hold a lot of blood, and an injury like his would create massive bleeding. We searched the park but found nothing. We completed our crime-scene work and went on to other tasks. It took a few minutes to confirm that the dead man was a Mr. P., a Filipino man in his late fifties, a cook at a nearby restaurant who had worked until just a few hours before his body was found. We spoke to his co-workers, who said he was on the telephone at about three in the morning. After he hung up, he told them he had a problem and left. He said he would return. We spoke to his family, but no one had a clue why anyone would want to kill Mr. P.—he was such a nice man. The investigation went nowhere, and after several months the case was shelved pending further investigation.

Two years later, I was sitting at my desk when I got a telephone call from a woman who spoke with a Filipino accent.

"Excuse me, sir, do you remember the murder of Mr. P. two years ago?"

"Yes, I do."

"I have to tell you. I see Mr. P.'s ghost."

Oh, great, I thought, *just what I need. A ghost.* But I had to be polite, and I asked the woman to tell me about it. As she spoke, I continued with my paperwork, with the telephone pinched between my shoulder and ear.

"I see Mr. P.'s ghost every time at Mrs. P.'s old business. Sometimes I smell his hair pomade before I see him."

"Where do you see him?" I asked, to be polite.

"Sometimes I see him in the office sitting at the desk. But most of the time, I see him at the bottom of the stairs, in the same spot where I saw Mrs. P. and her boyfriend cleaning the floor on the day Mr. P. was killed."

"What?" She had my attention now.

"I see him at the bottom of the stairs."

"What about Mrs. P. and her boyfriend?"

"The day Mr. P. was killed, I came work a little early. When I go inside, I see Mrs. P. and her boyfriend cleaning the floor at the bottom of the stairs. Mrs. P. tell me to go outside. She call me when can come in. Later that morning, policeman come and say Mr. P. was killed."

Okay, she had my *full* attention, now. We learned that Mrs. P. had sold her dress manufacturing business about six months ago. The employees, all Filipino women, were retained by the new owner. I spoke to the new owner. She gave us permission to come to the business and conduct an investigation.

We planned to search for blood using the new Luminol technique. To be safe, we obtained a search warrant first. We arrived at the business at dusk and met with the new owner, who was very cooperative, and the woman who claimed to see Mr. P.'s ghost. We served the warrant and explained that we were going to conduct Luminol testing because we thought that Mr. P. may have been killed at the business and taken to Ke'ehi Lagoon. The owner gave us the keys and asked that we lock up when we were finished. The woman who called me seemed very nervous. I asked her if something was wrong.

"Yes, sir."

"What is it?" I asked.

"I see Mr. P."

"Where?" I asked.

"He is standing right next to you."

I didn't see anyone, but that didn't keep the goose bumps from covering my neck, and it didn't stop me from moving away.

Luminol testing is not difficult. The chemical is mixed into a liquid form and placed into an aerosol sprayer. A camera is set up to photograph the results. Contrary to what you see on some TV shows, Luminol testing must be conducted in total darkness. Any light interferes with the observation of the results. The test involves luminescence, which is light without heat. The Luminol reaction involves chemiluminescence, which is light produced by a chemical reaction. The reaction creates chemical energy, which is converted into a blue light.

To photograph the results, the camera is set up on a tripod and fixed at the desired location. A photo is taken using regular lighting conditions. The film is not advanced. The lights are turned off and the Luminol is sprayed. If a reaction occurs, a blue chemiluminescence appears where the blood once was. The camera's shutter is opened and the blue light is allowed to burn into the film for about a minute. This method produces a photo that shows both the Luminol chemiluminescence and the background features.

We turned off the lights. We turned on the lights. Everyone was a little embarrassed at being spooked by the woman's comment that she could see Mr. P.'s ghost among us. We laughed and joked and turned off the lights again. It was really dark.

We applied the Luminol. The first area of the floor we applied the chemical to didn't produce any results. We moved to a new location nearer the wall and applied the Luminol again. This time, we got a bright blue chemiluminescence reaction, which we photographed.

We got similar reactions at different locations on the floor right up to the wall. The next step was simple. We removed the wall. Inside the wall we found a layer of dried blood, which we collected.

We sent the blood to a DNA Lab on the East Coast and the results indicated a match with the blood sample taken from Mr. P.'s body. We had our murder scene. And we had our suspects.

When we deal with people, even people who see ghosts, we should show respect. Remember the homicide detective I mentioned in chapter 18 who brushed off the witness to a murder at a Waipahu bar? About a week after the incident he *voluntarily* moved to another detail before that decision was made publicly for him.

Another detective, who was also an assistant football coach at a private high school, couldn't get his priorities straight and went to a football game, abandoning his partner at a homicide scene. He moved from the detail shortly thereafter as well.

Dedication is an absolute must for homicide detectives. And sometimes, homicide detectives expect absolute dedication from other officers and ancillary personnel as well. Gilbert Chang, the director of the Crime Lab, conducted blood analyses for us. Evidence specialists would recover the blood samples, we would write the requests for analysis, and Gilbert would analyze them. He was very dedicated—dedicated to the department and dedicated to his profession. In addition, Gilbert was just about the gentlest and most generous man you could ever know. If you needed something, Gilbert would give it to you, even if he had to bring it from his house the next day.

Every so often, the blood sample we had was small, and we would get back a report from Gilbert saying, "Insufficient amount collected to conduct analysis." This type of report usually brought a loud response from the detective: "F—king Gilbert." Now there wasn't a glut of "Insufficient Amount" reports from Gilbert, but he was the convenient scapegoat when blood work the detectives depended on didn't go the way they planned. Therefore the exclamation "F—king Gilbert." It happened often enough, though, that the detectives joked

The Crime Lab at 1455 S. Beretania Street in the early seventies

to Gilbert that he had a new name, "F—king Gilbert." Occasionally, when they saw him in the hallway, they would call out "Hey, F—king Gilbert, how's it going?" Like anyone else would, Gilbert played along and was amused by the joke for a little while. But after a while it got stale and overused, and Gilbert got annoyed.

One day, we were sent to an apartment in the Kāheka area where a woman who worked as a prostitute had been murdered. She was slashed to death with a razorlike instrument. We believed that the suspect held her against the wall as he slashed her, because blood spatter was everywhere on the wall except for where she stood against it. The outline of her body could be clearly seen. Because of the quantity of blood and the proximity of the police station to the scene, we asked Gilbert to come to the crime scene and supervise the collection of blood. He did, and many vials of blood were collected. The lead detective submitted his request for blood work, and in a few days we got Gilbert's report: "Insufficient amount collected to conduct analysis."

The detective went berserk. How could there be an insufficient amount collected to conduct an analysis? Gilbert himself supervised the collection. The detective charged upstairs to Gilbert's lab. I went with him to keep his temper under control. We hit the buzzer and the door was unlocked electronically. The detective rushed into Gilbert's office. Gilbert was sitting at his desk with a huge smile on his face. He was holding a fairly thick lab report.

"Here's your blood analysis report. That first report was payback for all the times I was called F—king Gilbert. Now knock it off." He laughed for days.

• • • • •

Most of the homicide detectives I worked with combined a sense of professionalism, a deep caring about the victims of the crimes we investigated, and a sense of humor in an all-too-grim job. I want to recognize the great men (there were no women in the detail then) who dedicated their lives to the investigation of the murder of other human beings. I wish to especially thank the detectives who worked with me during my tour of duty in the homicide detail: Rufus Kaukani, Andy Glushenko, John Isabelo, Paul Putzulu, Anderson Hee, Vernon Santos, Earl Hirai, James Kinimaka, Steve Dung, and Cliff Rubio. They brought different talents and backgrounds to a difficult, demanding, and often depressing job. They taught me about people, about investigation, and about teamwork. While we didn't always agree on the exact path to take to get there, we could all count on each other to do the right thing at the right time for the right reason, the first time.

34
The Media

A special relationship exists between the police and the media. It developed out of the public's concern about crime-related issues—a natural focal point for the media. This crime-related relationship is easily misconstrued by the police, who think the media are determined to make the police look bad. Here are some situations in which the police feel they are unfairly criticized by the media.

- When fear grips the community as a result of an upsurge in crime, or a crime spree, the media report it and turn to the police to see what is—or is not—being done.
- If the police are not making progress in a case, the media ask why.
- If police officials seem less than candid, the media comment about it.
- If officers are involved in misconduct, the media report it fully.

What the police fail to understand is that it is the professional and ethical obligation of journalists to inform the public and hold public officials accountable, whether they are police or politicians. The media have characterized themselves as the Fourth Estate. The other three are the executive, legislative, and judicial branches of government. Since the media interact on a daily basis with all branches of government at all levels—local, state, and federal—they establish themselves as the watchdogs for the community. What the police do and how they do it are subject to constant monitoring, and public opinion about crime and criminals is substantially influenced by the media.

There are four important facts about the police-media relationship:

1. The police feel that they are often the subject of biased coverage and sensationalism from the media.
2. The media feel that the police have been unduly closemouthed regarding issues about which the public *has the right to know*.
3. The public learns about crime and policing issues, including police misconduct, from the media.
4. The police and the media need each other.

What appears to be a simple relationship is actually more complicated than it looks. That police cultivate a good relationship with the media is important. It makes sense that this is the most logical way to keep the public informed of what's happening with the police and the community. When the police avoid publicity, or when reporters violate police sensibilities regarding media ethics, problems arise. The issue of the public's right to know is at the center of many police-media conflicts.

Interestingly enough, however, the U.S. Constitution does not provide for any such right. In addition, the U.S. Supreme Court has never required the government to make unlimited disclosure to the media. I got into an argument one day with a reporter from Channel 2 News. He insisted that the public's right to know is in the First Amendment. Not wishing to appear on the news as HPD's babooze of the week, I let him leave thinking he was right. But the truth is, there is no such right in the First Amendment. The First Amendment gives the right to a free press, but that does not equate to the public's having "the right to know." The challenge here is to turn the natural police-media conflict to constructive ends and maximize cooperation in the public's interest. Police officers whose simple answer to media inquiries is "No comment" epitomize an uncooperative spirit. But this has been so throughout history. A hundred or so years ago, Lord Tyrrell, permanent undersecretary of the British Foreign Office, had this to say about the government's relationship with the media: "You think we lie to you, but we don't lie, really we don't. However, when you discover that, you make an even greater error. You think we tell you the truth."

Too many police officers subscribe to this philosophy. Tell the media something, but don't tell them the truth. This comes around to bite them later. When Chief Michael Nakamura took office, he believed that an open relationship with the media was necessary, and he had his command attend courses on how to deal with the media.

Developing a working relationship with the media was one thing. Having police officers who, for whatever reason, leaked information, true or otherwise, was something completely different. There was a high-ranking officer in CID who everyone knew was leaking information to the reporters. He was publicly proud of his news leaks. Whenever he disagreed with an administrative decision, he ran to the media. When he thought prosecutors were demanding too much in a case, he would run to the media. When he felt he needed an ego boost, he ran to the media. All for the wrong reasons. It was strange that he was never publicly reprimanded for his blatant violations of policy. Unfortunately, some reporters believed that he was an excellent source. You could tell when he leaked info to the media because "an unnamed police source" or "a police source who spoke only on condition of anonymity" was cited.

Crime is the natural focus of the media, and homicide is one of the offenses that bring the police and the public together. In this context, I had many, many contacts with the media. Chief Nakamura wanted the CID lieutenants to provide the media with information on cases that became publicly newsworthy. All the homicides fit this bill, but the media were accustomed to hearing "No comment." Nakamura wanted the public to hear about and see the efforts of our officers and detectives as they worked the robberies and homicides. It was quite possible to provide the media with information on a homicide, for example, without giving them any confidential information. Instead of coming out of a homicide crime scene with a "No comment," it was perfectly okay to tell reporters that we were working on a homicide: that a thirty-five-year-old male was found dead in his house of apparent gunshot wounds, that police have not yet identified a suspect, but are working on the case, and so forth. Some officers would say we're releasing too much information by saying that the man died of apparent gunshot wounds. I disagree. We're not telling the reporters what kind of gun, or where the injuries were on the victim's body. Some officers don't think police officers should speak to reporters at all. They think it's a violation of honor or creed. After all, aren't the media our enemy?

Only when they show us falling down in the rain. I went to a homicide case in Wahiawā. It was storming. The murder occurred in a house down a steep driveway. I fell down on the driveway and slid about six feet on my backside. It made the ten o'clock news. I've never been known as a vindictive man, but, at the next homicide, that TV cameramen had better have lenses that can shoot 90 degrees around corners.

We should have a working relationship with the media so that when we fall on a slippery driveway, it does not make the news. Reporters, cameramen, and the police should not engage in activities to trick the other. A cameraman from one of the top-rated television stations would point his camera at the ground, indicating to the unsuspecting police officer that it was off, then say to the officer, "Come on, what really happened?" Actually, the camera was on and running and recording the voice of the damn fool who was providing this "nice guy" with all the information on the case. The officer's information usually showed up on the news as a voiceover from an "anonymous police source," while video of the crime scene played.

I felt I had a good working relationship with the media. It was based on respect and an understanding that we both needed to do our jobs as professionally as possible.

Three basic principles lay the foundation for a good police-media relationship.

1. Establish a clear policy as to the type of information that can be released to the media and the procedures for that release.
2. Treat all reporters objectively, equally, and fairly.
3. Be as open as possible, to meet the public's right to know; at the same time, maintain appropriate confidentiality of information about victims, witnesses, and suspects.

The Honolulu Police Department has the appropriate policies and procedures for dealing with the media and releasing information. The proper execution of those policies is the responsibility of all officers.

35
Prosecutors and Courts

One of the most frustrating issues for any detective is to have conducted a top-notch investigation that took long hours of hard work only to have the suspect plead to a lesser offense in court. This may be even more exasperating in a homicide investigation, because when the detective finishes the case, he's absolutely sure that the suspect committed the murder. When the suspect pleads to manslaughter, the detective is so angry he can pop. He's angry with the courts, he's angry with the prosecutors. A murderer got away with a lesser offense.

This is the trap that some officers fall into. They view their hard work as having only one outcome—prosecution for the offense they charged the defendant with. As they learn more about criminal justice and our judicial system, officers realize that they are only one cog in this wheel of justice. When an officer grieves about a case and says he worked his heart out and did the best investigation he could, he should be praised for that hard work, because that's his job— that's his function in the system of criminal justice. Then it is up to the prosecutors to do their best work.

The prosecutors have many issues to face, and the first is the courts. Within the judicial system, one group that has very few backers and very few supporters is the courts. Every year, more and more cases appear in front of the few judges who must hear these cases. Year after year in the legislature, the judges fail to get the support they need to hear this increase in cases. It's a vicious cycle. The community demands that the police keep crime down. The police use every tactic available to them to accomplish this, including increased arrests and citations. These cases then go to the courts as increased caseloads, and the system bogs down. So the courts and prosecutors use another tactic to keep cases flowing through the system—plea bargains.

A plea bargain is the acceptance of a lesser plea by the prosecutors and courts in order to obtain a guilty plea and verdict without having to go to court. Some officers think prosecutors don't give enough thought to the work put into a case. But they do. Prosecutors review the circumstances of the case, the completeness of the investigation, the level of evidence available to prove the case, the criminal history of the defendant, and the outcome of a potential case versus a plea bargain. If a plea bargain will serve the community without jeopardizing the community then perhaps it is better to keep the system flowing and save the effort and money a trial would cost. In many cases, the defendant is sent to prison anyway, perhaps for a lesser offense. He is off the streets for the time being, and prison may rehabilitate him.

Plea bargains are quite different from deals made with suspects. I always had a hard time accepting deals. I thought the suspect was using the system to his advantage by ratting out a criminal colleague. One day we were sent to a homicide involving a motorcyclist who was shot in a drug deal gone bad. The motorcyclist witnessed the drug robbery, and one of the suspects fired a shot as the motorcyclist sped away, hitting him in the back of the head. Lucky shot. The best clue in the investigation was the statement given by the drug dealer, who identified the robbers. Most of the time, people who rob drug dealers are the drug dealer's clients. That was the case here. The dealer gave them up with very little prodding.

All three suspects were brought in for questioning. One of the three was extremely nervous and wanted to "talk" to us. "Talk" he did, but he didn't confess. He talked about "talking" only if he was given a deal. He would tell us who the shooter was if he was given immunity from prosecution. Then the conflict arose. The prosecutors would give him a deal only if he took a polygraph exam (lie detector test) to show that he was telling the truth. The suspect refused the polygraph. But since the other suspects weren't talking, this one guy was quickly becoming a key witness. He got his immunity. He ratted out the shooter. The shooter then wanted to talk. He ratted out the first suspect as being the shooter, not him. But the first suspect already had immunity. Oh-oh. Who's telling the truth? The guy with immunity or the guy accused as being the shooter? The third suspect didn't need to talk now. He may have been involved in the robbery, but he wasn't implicated in the murder by either of his drug-using *cumpades.*

Messes like this don't normally happen. Usually there is sufficient evidence to corroborate the statement given for the deal, and usually the suspect agrees to a polygraph.

The prosecutor becomes involved with the homicide investigation early on. Usually, one prosecutor is assigned to hear the investigation status and give advice. I wish we could take this one step further and have a prosecutor come to the crime scene for a firsthand look at the evidence and witnesses. Some argue that the prosecutor might then try to steer the direction of the investigation. I don't agree with that argument. If the prosecutor knows that his or her place is to advise at the scene, we should have few problems. It would be better for the community, the family of the murdered victim, and the investigation if the prosecutors were on site when the crime scene is investigated. Lack of resources, unfortunately, has prevented this in the past.

Having a prosecutor at the crime scene would be helpful when we decide whether to videotape the crime scene. There are arguments for and against videotaping. Here are a few points:

For videotaping:
- It provides a nonstatic, color representation of the crime scene.
- It can portray the scene in a continuous view.
- It portrays the scene in real time.

Against videotaping:
- What is portrayed is confined by the width of the lens and is dependent upon the photographer's point of view.

- The portrayal of the scene can be manipulated.
- Background conversations can be detrimental to the neutrality of the investigator.

We videotaped a few cases and used the tapes for training purposes. In one instance we had the photographer comment, "Will you look at that shit!" Another photographer commented to a detective on the beauty of one of the female officers protecting the crime scene. Neither photographer realized that what he was saying was being recorded on the videotape.

I tried my hand at it. We were sent to a murder in Pearl City; a young man stabbed his friend to death. The suspect was asleep in his house. His friend entered and woke him from a deep sleep. Startled and thinking that he was being attacked by someone he didn't know, he grabbed a knife and stabbed the friend. Or so he said. We doubted him. For one thing, the killing occurred in broad daylight. We also knew that the two had been involved in drug deals that had gone bad, and that they had argued.

I grabbed the video camera and began to tape the exterior of the scene. This camera was not one of the small hand-held cameras used today. This was a big, bulky model that rested on one shoulder and used a full-sized VHS tape. I felt good about my taping. I showed both sides of the house and street and proceeded to walk through the gate around the back with one eye closed and the other peering through the viewfinder. As I turned the corner, I was describing the scenery. I turned and moved along the side of the house. That's when I woke the pit bull. He jumped up. I focused on him and began to move quickly away. The pit bull was not tied to anything. His demonic look said, *GET OUT!* But he didn't wait to see if I was getting out. He thought my leg was a better attraction. I knew that if he bit me, I would be in a world of hurt, so I hit him with the camera. I don't remember, but I must have been crying out for help because an officer came to my aid. The dog shook his head and looked at me with eyes that said, *Oh, I'm going to make you sorry for doing that!* As I backed out the gate, I used the camera as a shield, blocking the dog as the officer alternately sprayed the dog and me with Mace.

Later, when we looked at the tape, we could clearly hear me swearing above the barking of the dog. We couldn't see much because the lens was swinging wildly, but we could hear me say, "Hey, watch where you're spraying that damn Mace." It was obvious that my first attempt at producing, directing, and filming that crime scene would not be introduced at the Cannes Film Festival.

More important, I was beginning to wonder what was it with me and dogs.

36
Scientific Investigation Section

In 1988, when I attended a homicide seminar at the FBI Academy in Quantico, Virginia, I met detectives from Florida's Dade County and we discussed a cold case squad they developed at their department. I was interested because notable cases in Honolulu were just sitting on shelves because investigators were unable to convince prosecutors to file charges against the suspects. I hoped to bring Dade County's experience home to HPD and develop a squad of our own.

When I returned, I presented the proposal to my superiors. The chief supported the concept, and all we needed was budget approval to bring two more detectives into the Homicide Detail to reopen old murders, reexamine evidence, reinterview witnesses, speak to suspects, if possible, and try to develop enough proof to take the cases back to the prosecutors. The reexamination of evidence was critical, to determine if new techniques could be applied to the old evidence.

We got the budgetary approval, and two new detectives were brought into the detail. It was my hope that this team would look at some of the major unsolved murder cases: Lisa Au, Diane Suzuki, and the serial killings of the mid-eighties, to name a few, and perhaps bring charges against the killers. During my time with the Homicide Detail, we were not successful in solving those major cases, but the team was able to close several murders based on their reexaminations.

Much to my chagrin, a new major in CID wanted me out as the homicide lieutenant. He wanted to replace me with a lieutenant who was a friend of his. This was a frustrating time. I had hoped to leave the detail by being promoted to captain. I had scored high on the exam and thought I did well in the interview process. But there appeared to be a battle of sorts between the new major, who was trying to expand his own power base, and the chief, who was trying to get the major to realize that he was under the chief's command and therefore subject to the chief's desires. I supported the chief and began to feel the strain of being in the middle, so I asked the chief if I could leave the detail. I was transferred to the Scientific Investigation Section (SIS) as its lieutenant.

The Scientific Investigation Section was the brainchild of Captain Wilson Sullivan. He took the old Evidence Technician Detail of the Records Division and developed it into the unit it is today. Sullivan was a great field expert who encouraged his evidence specialists to rise to new levels of expertise. When he was promoted to major of the Research and Development Division, I was promoted to replace him as captain of the Scientific Investigation Section.

There was little I could do to improve the expertise of the evidence specialists, but there was a lot to do in the area of community interaction. Chief Michael Nakamura challenged his division commanders to find new ways to bring the police to the public and to interact with the community. When I thought about the name of our unit, the only science I could relate it to was my old high school science classes. So my natural response was to do something with and for high school students: a science fair tailored to law enforcement— a Forensic Science Fair. It caught the eye of the Department of Education, and in the three years that we held the fair at HPD, it grew from twelve entries to nearly fifty. Several entries were winners in the State Science Fair as well. Some of our students won college and university scholarships.

As an adjunct activity to the science fair, we began a Forensic Science Club for middle and high school students. Club members met monthly to discuss science topics related to law enforcement. These activities attracted the interest of a few DOE science teachers, and before we knew it our high school science activities made it to DOE TV specials.

In 1992, when the author was with the Scientific Investigation Section, the department moved to its present headquarters on Beretania Street.

But these activities were designed for students only. We needed a project for adults. While visiting San Francisco I attended a theater performance in which the audience interacted with the actors to solve a mystery. Using that concept, I developed the Sherlock Holmes Night. I wrote a short mystery that was sent to the people who planned to participate. On the night of the event, we had interactive booths displaying forensic science fields of study such as chemical analysis, blood analysis, trace evidence, latent fingerprint evidence, and crime-scene investigation. One big attraction was that media celebrities acted out the mystery, bringing the characters to life. The first Sherlock Holmes Night was held at the police headquarters courtyard. Five hundred people participated that first night. Six years later we presented the event at the Blaisdell Exhibition Hall, and more than two thousand people attended. It was through Sherlock Holmes Night that I introduced two fictional private investigators, Perryleen Mason and Waltah Babooze, in a series of short mysteries: *Who Threw Stanley into the Volcano? Who Chopped Chang?* and *Who Poisoned Waltah Babooze?*

After I retired, I was thrilled to see the department continue Sherlock Holmes Night. It's a way to bring the public in to see just what police investigations involve and to learn a little about forensic science.

An area of SIS that people know little about is the Crime Lab, because the work is conducted mainly inside the police headquarters. During the time that I was at SIS, the Crime Lab was divided into four areas: Chemical Analysis, Blood Lab, Documents, and Trace Evidence. It's the job of lab technicians in these departments to analyze the evidence that comes from the crime scene. The Blood Lab area will soon be able to conduct its own DNA testing. You may remember learning about DNA, a chemical building block otherwise known as deoxyribonucleic acid, in your high school science courses. DNA evidence is now a crucial tool in criminal investigations. The department currently sends samples for DNA analysis to a mainland lab, but with the advent of its own capabilities in Honolulu, HPD will save time and money.

After a tour in SIS, I was assigned briefly to the Informational Resources Section. This section, formerly called community relations, came directly under the chief and was responsible for special projects, community interaction, Neighborhood Watch, the No Hope in Dope program, and the Police Museum.

Then one day I got a call from Chief Mike Nakamura saying that I was being promoted to the rank of major. With all my experience in criminal investigation, I thought I was a shoo-in to be the new CID major, an assignment I really wanted. I would be working in an area I knew, with people I respected, building on projects we had started and creating new ones.

"Gary, congratulations, I'm promoting you to major," the chief said cheerily.

I exhaled. I had slightly more than twenty-five years with the department at that time. Yet suddenly, I was thinking back to my early days as a recruit, when I never would have dreamed that I would one day hold the rank of major.

"Thank you, sir," I said, waiting for him to give me the assignment to CID.

"You're replacing Barbara Wong in Traffic Division," he said.

"Sir," I said. *Shit,* I thought.

37
On Being a Major

When I was a rookie, we looked upon majors as demigods. The gods themselves (assistant chiefs and up) were housed on the second floor of the old department building. The majors, however, were the commanders of the divisions. They were the elders of the department, to quote Mike Nakamura. They were older officers. They were wiser officers. They ran the show. They were awe-inspiring.

But when I was promoted to the rank of major, I didn't feel that anyone held me in awe. Nor did I feel old—I was forty-six. And as for feeling wiser? Nope. I did feel more responsible for the people who worked for me, and I suddenly realized that when the gods asked for an accounting, it would be me that they held accountable.

The first thing a new major is greeted with is the skepticism of the rank and file within the division. *Here we go again—and we were just getting used to the other guy. What's this new guy going to be like?* Everyone is worried that the new major will try to impress the A/Cs with new programs and new projects that will have to be carried out by the line troops. And they were right. My pet project was to ensure that people who killed people with their cars were properly charged and held responsible for their actions.

Being a major meant that now I was a demigod. But something had happened in the twenty-five years since I was a young officer. That power had shifted somewhat from the majors to the assistant chiefs. The majors did not have the final say on many things. That final decision came from above. And not necessarily from the assistant chiefs. Often, items had to go even further up the chain to the deputies and the chief himself. (I often thought that decisions went so high because of our own reluctance to be responsible and accountable for our own decisions and because of some poor decisions made by some commanders along the way.) We were now more like caretakers of the division until the next guy came along.

The majors did have the authority to develop projects and programs. So I felt empowered to pursue my goals concerning negligent homicide.

One aspect of being a major that I was not particularly fond of was the Wednesday morning staff meeting. We met with our respective assistant chiefs every morning at 7:30 for news, information, and instructions, but every Wednesday morning there was a staff meeting for all division commanders. Here, each division commander reported on the status of his or her division and special projects. For some reason, I felt uncomfortable in this setting. On occasion, a commander would get up and praise his division. And then another, and then another. To me it became too much of a dog-and-pony show. To try to make the meetings more meaningful, Chief Nakamura instructed each commander to discuss the status of his or her division, not just report on commendations.

Every once in a while something special happened at those Wednesday meetings. One day I remember in particular. Those meetings could run long and they were uncomfortable to sit through after a few cups of coffee. So I planned ahead and made sure I used the restroom beforehand. When we settled in at the meeting, the chief made an announcement.

"All of us will be taking part in a urinalysis drug test. We cannot expect the line troops to participate in such testing unless the command staff also participate. Obviously, the announcement had to be a surprise to you all."

Obviously, my empty bladder whined. There was absolutely no way I would be able to produce a sample in the next hour or two. A few of us stood around the water fountain next to the restroom where the testing was taking place, alternately taking turns and drinking as much water as our bellies could hold.

"Any luck?" asked the IA lieutenant.

Three of us shook our heads.

"Well, sirs, you have forty-five minutes more and then we will need to turn this test in with a report of your inability to participate." One of the rules associated with the urinalysis was that the subject has to provide a sample within a certain time.

The water fountain poured out more water. Normally I really like ice-cold water, but I drank so much in that hour it didn't taste good anymore.

"You know, a beer would help," suggested one of the other majors.

We eventually provided the sample they were looking for. Welcome to the administration.

· · · · ·

The Traffic Division I now commanded was made up of three units: Traffic Fatality Investigation, Solo Bike Detail, and the Junior Police Officers (JPO) Detail. The JPO Detail provides police support to schools that have Junior Police Officers. They help direct traffic at schools and provide a police presence to the school and the surrounding neighborhoods. The police also provide security to the children arriving and leaving the schoolgrounds.

The Solo Bike Detail's main responsibility is to provide support to the morning and afternoon highway traffic. The officers cruise the freeways and main thoroughfares such as the Kalaniana'ole, Pali, and Likelike highways during peak traffic hours to move stalled vehicles and traffic collisions out of the way of the traffic flow. During non-traffic hours, the solo bikes assist the various patrol districts by looking for traffic code violators. Yes, these are our friends in the police department who carry more than one tag book at a time.

The Traffic Fatality Investigation Detail, formerly known as TAIS, Traffic Accident Investigation Section, is responsible for investigating all traffic fatalities, known as negligent homicides. It was here that I brought my homicide investigation background into play. In my mind, the problem with negligent homicides lay in the intent of the perpetrators.

For every offense in the penal code, one part of the *corpus delicti,* or the elements of the crime, is the intent of the perpetrator. Each crime has one level of intent attached to it, as defined in the Hawai'i Penal Code:

- Intentionally: A person acts intentionally with respect to his conduct when it is his *conscious object* to engage in such conduct.
- Knowingly: A person acts knowingly with respect to his conduct when he *is aware* that his conduct is of that nature.
- Recklessly: A person acts recklessly with respect to his conduct when he *consciously disregards* a substantial and unjustifiable risk that the person's conduct is of the specified nature.
- Negligently: A person acts negligently with respect to his conduct when he *should be aware* of a substantial and unjustifiable risk taken that the person's conduct is of the specified nature.

My argument has always been with the Negligent level of intent. I cannot agree that the phrase describing negligence, *should be aware*, represents the actions of some drivers who kill people in collisions. For example, you *should be aware* that by reaching to turn down your radio and taking your eyes off the road you are being negligent. Compare that example to someone speeding. A person driving at high speed, in my opinion at least, *consciously disregards* a substantial and unjustifiable risk, or acts recklessly. The same is true for people who drive drunk.

When a person who was speeding or driving drunk kills another person in a collision, his or her action was reckless, not negligent, at least in my mind. His or her actions recklessly caused the death of another. That is manslaughter, not negligent homicide.

Another problem I have with that section of the penal code is that under certain conditions you can kill another person through negligent homicide and be guilty of only a misdemeanor. I just don't believe that one human being can take the life of another, even through negligence, and be guilty of only a misdemeanor. I wonder what our legislators had in mind when they approved this? Perhaps, because our society is so automobile based, some lawmakers are willing to accept that an occasional human being is going to get knocked off every so often.

My pet project was to review each negligent homicide and, when I believed we had a case—when I believed that the driver's actions were reckless, not negligent—the investigators were instructed to present the case to the prosecutors as manslaughter. We didn't win agreement from the prosecutors on all the cases brought forward, but we were successful in some cases and in educating investigators to be alert to the driver's actions and charge defendants accordingly.

Because the death of a person in a traffic case is a violation of the penal code—that is, a criminal offense—the crime scene is the location of the collision, whatever roadway it occurred on. We refer to these deaths as traffic fatalities, as if they were somewhat less important than other homicides. The death of a person in a traffic collision is equally horrific, and the subsequent investigation should be equally thorough and complete. Investigating a crime scene is no longer a cakewalk. It requires intensive scrutiny. And there's the catch. When traffic fatalities are investigated, people are going to be inconvenienced and won't be happy about it. Let me give you an example.

On the morning of August 8, 1997, at 8:15, an eleven-year-old girl named Katie McKenzie was walking with her father along King Street. Attorney Jerry Wilson was driving on Bishop Street. Wilson's car went out of control, sped across the intersection, climbed the sidewalk, and struck Katie. She suffered critical injuries and lay near death for several days. At about the same time, a murder occurred near Beretania and Smith streets. Both intersections were closed off while these investigations took place. No one complained about the murder investigation, but there were several gripes that the police were taking too long on the traffic *accident*. Was it an accident? Was there negligence involved? Or recklessness? Would Katie live? (Fortunately, she did.) Hurry up guys, someone needs to get to the office.

The author in 1997 as the major in charge of the Traffic Division

Some people may never think the investigation of a traffic death is as important as the investigation of a murder. It doesn't help when the mayor of the city is among those complaining that it takes too long to investigate a traffic death. One morning, Mayor Jeremy Harris was caught in a traffic jam because police were investigating the death of a man who was killed riding a motorcycle on the freeway. Apparently the people who complained that morning along with the mayor felt that since the accident victim was alone, police should just sweep up the pieces of him and his bike and haul it away. What's the message? That'll teach him for speeding? What if he was run off the road? Or what if the road had a defect that contributed to his death? But never mind, we're late for the office.

Yes, my sarcasm gets the best of me from time to time, but I can never understand how people can argue for a less thorough investigation of a death caused by someone who may have been acting recklessly or negligently.

For those who get perturbed at having to endure a traffic jam because the police are investigating the killing of another person by a reckless or negligent driver, I have a suggestion. Think of someone you love. Then think of that person being killed because of the reckless or negligent action of someone else. Think of how you never got to say goodbye. Then think how important it is for the police to get every bit of evidence and information they can in order to bring justice to the killer of the person you love—and maybe stop them from killing someone else. If you can still tell the police, "Hurry up, damn it, I'm late," take the next left and try another route.

38
Integrity

I rounded out my career in the Traffic Division. It was a challenging assignment, involving ongoing traffic and personnel issues. Perhaps the biggest mistake I made there involved enforcement of the diamond-lane restrictions during morning rush-hour traffic.

The diamond lane, also known as the HOV (high-occupancy vehicle) or carpool lane, is reserved for vehicles with two or more occupants during the morning and afternoon rush hours. Because it's dangerous for officers to pull over vehicles on the freeway, the rules for use of the diamond lane were rarely enforced. Because of that lack of enforcement, the number of people ignoring the rules rose steadily. A State Department of Transportation (DOT) study found that more than half of the diamond-lane users were violators. We got a call one day from a DOT representative who asked for help in the diamond-lane enforcement. He suggested that officers go out early in the morning to the Pearl City area of the H-1 freeway and, from a position behind a median barrier, write down the license-plate numbers of violators. Tags would be written up and mailed to the registered owners of the vehicles in violation of the code.

I presented this proposal to the administration. Feedback was mixed. Some thought we would get a large number of complaints. I thought the effort would be more positive than negative, and I was given permission to proceed.

The target area was the H-1 freeway's eastbound diamond lane, directly under the Kaonohi Street overpass. The plan was simple. DOT would block a lane of westbound traffic for use by officers. The lane would be coned for one mile approaching the operation site, and several large trucks would be positioned so that no driver could—accidentally or deliberately—swerve into the officers.

Not even I wanted to sneak up on the motorists, so HPD and DOT conducted a media blitz warning drivers of the impending diamond-lane checks and tags. For more than a week, the media put out warnings. We enlisted the aid of several popular morning-drive radio celebrities on AM and FM radio stations. In TV ads and newspaper articles, DOT warned drivers not to violate the diamond lane. Even on the morning that enforcement began, major radio stations were broadcasting that the police would be out looking for diamond-lane violators. By all accounts, everyone knew we were coming.

Our officers were in place by 6:00 a.m. By 6:30, traffic was backed up to the H-2. By 7:00, traffic was backed up past Waikele. By 7:30, Wai'anae motorists had nowhere to go. Traffic approaching the officers slowed to a crawl. This slowing of traffic created a gridlock preventing the diamond-lane violators from escaping the lane when they saw the officers.

We issued several hundred citations to diamond-lane violators. DOT made its point. The state made lots of money from the traffic citations. And we created the largest traffic jam in anyone's memory.

Complaints about foul-ups of this nature, while supporting the theory that traffic enforcement is the most negative contact people have with the police, are fairly easy to deal with. Complaints about officers who shirk their duties and evade their responsibilities are much more difficult to handle.

During the year I was in charge of the Traffic Division, on several occasions my boss told me that during his ride to work in the morning, he didn't see any solo bike officers. His observations revealed a pattern: the days my boss didn't see any officers were the days a particular sergeant and his crew were assigned to the morning traffic.

I assigned the lieutenant in charge of the Solo Bike Detail to investigate. On some days, the officers were out in force. On other days, he couldn't find them. Maybe it was a coincidence that they

The solo motorcycle squad (1997)

weren't around when he was driving the freeways—or maybe it wasn't. He used our police helicopter to search on several different mornings. He couldn't find the officers who were supposed to be on the freeways.

Word of our efforts to locate the missing squad must have reached the patrol officers in town, because we soon received information that our officers were holed up in the old police radio shop at the former headquarters on Beretania Street in Pawa'a. This location was currently used as a motorcycle club by department members and retirees who rode motorcycles for fun. The squad we were looking for was led by a veteran sergeant. I felt sure that his men could not escape their morning assignment without his knowing.

More disappointed than angry, I again assigned the solo bike lieutenant to investigate. He came into my office later that morning and shut my door. He told me that he arrived at the old radio shop about thirty minutes after the officers were to hit the road for the morning traffic assignment—well before sunup. The roll-up door to the shop was down. He watched until eight o'clock and saw no activity. As he was about to leave, the door rolled up and four solo bike officers emerged—the sergeant and three members of his squad. They had apparently been in the shop from the time they were supposed to hit the road until just after eight, when their freeway assignment was over. The lieutenant made no effort to stop them. Instead, he came to me and reported his findings.

Once again, I was more disappointed than angry.

Since most of that sergeant's squad were involved, I took the issue to Internal Affairs. My old beat partner Russell was now the lieutenant in charge of investigations. After I discussed the case with him, he assigned a team of detectives to investigate.

The IA staff set up a van directly outside the door of the radio shop. In the van was a detective with a video camera. Other detectives were placed nearby to observe activity. For one week, like clockwork, that senior sergeant led his squad directly from their morning briefing to the radio shop. And they remained there each day until peak traffic subsided.

On the last day of the IA investigation, I went to the shop, confronted the sergeant, and ordered him to report to my office. His officers were sent to their freeway assignments. I was not surprised that the sergeant thought I was picking on him and thought I should have given him a warning instead of giving the case to IA. His misguided sense of responsibility brought down the officers under his command and tarnished their badges and reputations as well. Those involved were disciplined and transferred.

It was particular y sad to see this incident among members of the Solo Bike Detail. The officers of the bike squad perform duties that are extraordinarily dangerous. They help investigate traffic fatalities, protect visiting dignitaries, and keep the traffic flowing during the worst time to be riding a bike on our freeways. They speak to our school children about traffic safety and serve as role models.

I was leaving the force in a few weeks—retiring after nearly twenty-seven years of service to become the manager of security at

The Queen's Medical Center. While I was disappointed by the incident, I knew that the professional reputation of the solo bike officers would prevail.

39
There Is Life After Police Work

Many police officers fear the unknown that awaits them after a career with the police department. Of course, people leaving any career may have doubts and worries. But I really believe that retirement looms larger for police officers. They spend their careers in secure positions with fixed routines in jobs that provide built-in support groups and ready-made identities. Some officers never want to retire, afraid they won't know what to do with their time.

One case in point was the life and career of a detective named Joe Jones. Joe spent many, many years with the police department. When Joe came to the department, foot patrol officers didn't carry radios and had to rely on telephones on every other block to report in. When he left, the department was using sophisticated chemical techniques and tools to help solve crimes. Joe grew very old with the police department. He was a nice man, always smiling, always quick to tell a war story or two if you had the time to listen. When we spoke to Joe, we learned that he and his wife still lived in the old house. We learned that his two daughters had both died young and that he missed them very much. More important, we learned that Joe didn't have much of a life when he left work for the day.

He must have been in his seventies. He walked slowly, with a slight stoop. His hair had grown white over time. It was said that he served more than forty years with the department. Every so often, someone would ask, "Joe, why don't you retire and enjoy life?" I heard him reply often enough, "I don't have anything to do outside of police work. When I retire is when I'll die."

One day Joe agreed with the critics and said enough was enough. He finally retired. There was a big party. Joe seemed happy.

I don't remember exactly how long it was after Joe retired (but I do remember it wasn't long—a few months at most) when someone said, "Did you hear? Joe Jones died." I remember thinking that Joe must have known that his time was about up and he wanted his wife to have his retirement pension. In those days, if an officer was unfortunate enough to die before he retired, his surviving beneficiary got only what he contributed to the plan. His monthly pension was lost to his family.

We passed the hat and collected some money for Joe's widow. She sent us a thank-you note. And though it must have hurt to say it, she added: "Please don't be like Joe. Stop and smell the roses before it's too late." She was saying that there's more to life than just police work—recognize the opportunity and take advantage of it.

When I left the Homicide Detail, I felt a sense of loss. It had been important to me to help build a team that conducted professional investigations into the murders of innocent people. That sadness lasted only a few days before I came to grips with the fact that it was time to move to a new assignment and new responsibilities.

After my retirement, I missed the people I worked with every day, but the feeling of loss never came. I had had a good career, but it was time to move on. The prospect of being manager of the Security Department for The Queen's Medical Center was exciting. Queen's is the biggest and perhaps busiest hospital on O'ahu. It serves as the Trauma Center for the Pacific. Its reputation is excellent. Its security force does everything city cops do—without guns. I felt that, yes, there is life after police work.

In looking back over twenty-seven years, I am proud to have been a member of HPD during a time of change. I watched the department grow from a male-only profession to an agency that welcomes women as equals. I was able to serve under a variety of chiefs, ending with the one who perhaps did the most to break the barriers between the department and the community, Michael Nakamura. Our investigative tools and techniques advanced into areas I couldn't even imagine as a recruit. I served in a wide variety of assignments. And I am especially proud to have served as the lieutenant in charge of the Homicide Detail. I was part of the team working with Mike Nakamura to help open the locked door between the media and the police. The years were filled with extraordinarily dangerous and stressful events, exciting and adventurous times, and funny and ridiculous situations.

But through it all, one constant revealed itself time and again as the overwhelming reason that the Honolulu Police Department is considered among the best in the nation: the people who serve as officers, dispatchers, evidence specialists, and civilian workers.

So I left HPD and moved on to The Queen's Medical Center. With all the complexities associated with such a large trauma center and hospital, nearly fourteen acres, three thousand employees, and every type of case and issue associated with life in a big city, there was one training directive that I needed to make sure was given first.

Water and gasoline don't mix.

Postscript:
In the Line of Duty

They lined up three ranks deep on the sidewalk fronting the Beretania Street police station and the park adjacent to the building, their dark blue uniforms contrasting with the shades of white and gray of the concrete. Across the street an equally long line also gathered in three ranks. Mixed in and behind the uniforms on the sidewalk and grassy slopes of the park were civilian employees and members of the media. The flags in front of the police building were at half-mast. People were fidgeting. The heat coming off the concrete made it seem hotter than it was. The mood was somber and people spoke in hushed tones. Traffic flowed past with drivers and passengers staring and wondering what was going on. Then the traffic slowed and soon disappeared altogether. A voice boomed out, " 'Ten-hut!" The uniforms snapped to attention. The civilians stood still. "Present arms!" came the next command. The officers saluted.

The funeral procession of Officer Dannygriggs Padayao came into view and moved slowly down Beretania Street, passing the rows of officers standing at attention. HPD was burying one of its own, and the men and women of the department came to pay their last respects to the officer killed on April 30, 2001, by a person suspected of drunk driving. Six years earlier, a similar procession was held for Officers Bryant Bayne and Tate Kahakai, who died in a helicopter crash during a search-and-rescue mission for a lost hiker.

The last thing a police officer expects is to die on duty. He realizes that some situations can be extraordinarily dangerous, but he trusts in his training, his common sense, and the inner voice that tells him when something is wrong. He gets through the dangerous times. And he goes home. Except for the officers who, through the years, don't make it through those times.

As the funeral procession slowly passed you could see the questions in the eyes of many of the officers: *How many times did I put myself in the same dangerous situation as Danny did? How close has it come to being me, over the years?*

Death is as much a part of life as birth. We accept that one day we will die, that our existence will end. We hope our ending will be peaceful, after a long, joyful life.

But there is a special tragedy when a police officer dies in the line of duty. Or a firefighter, or others who devote themselves to serving society. It's not merely that the death was sudden and unexpected. It's that the life was taken away—stolen, if you will—from someone who was serving the community. It's as if the community lost a family member to a sudden, violent death. And it deeply affects the survivors of the organization. It's a time when officers examine themselves and their ability to do their work safely. It's a time when administrators examine guidelines, policies, and procedures, asking themselves if there is something that can be done to reduce the risk to officers. And it's a time of recommitment to the promise to protect and serve.

On the wall at the entrance to the police headquarters is a plaque. It lists the names of the officers who died in service to our community. While we may feel we can never do enough for the families of those who have fallen, the plaque is a permanent memorial to the supreme sacrifice of those officers.

As of this writing, these officers have fallen in the line of duty.

Non Omnis Moriar

Officer John W. Mahelona	November 19, 1903
Officer Manuel D. Abreu	November 7, 1913
Officer Frederick Wright	April 30, 1916
Officer James K. Keonaona	August 8, 1923
Officer David W. Mahukona	October 28, 1923
Officer Edwin H. Boyd	August 5, 1925
Officer George Macy	July 22, 1926
Officer Samson Paele	July 24, 1927
Detective William K. Kama	October 5, 1928
Officer George Rogers	September 10, 1930
Sergeant Henry A. Chillingworth	February 18, 1936
Officer Wah Choon Lee	August 3, 1937
Officer Alfred W. Dennis	May 2, 1942
Officer Joseph K. Whitford Jr.	October 28, 1963
Officer Abraham E. Mahiko	December 16, 1963
Officer Andrew R. Morales	December 16, 1963
Officer Patrick K. Ihu	June 1, 1964
Lieutenant Benedict Eleneki	October 21, 1964
Officer Bradley N. Kaanana	July 3, 1965
Officer Frank R. Medeiros	January 25, 1967
Reserve Officer Ernest G. Lindemann	October 30, 1969
Officer David R. Huber	June 20, 1971
Officer Robert A. Corter	October 4, 1975
Officer Larry J. Stewart	February 12, 1976
Pilot Thomas A. Moher	March 16, 1977

Officer Merlin C. Kaeo   March 16, 1977

Officer Ernest R. Grogg   August 26, 1979

Officer David W. Parker   March 1, 1985

Officer David N. Ronk   June 15, 1987

Officer Troy Barboza   October 22, 1987

Officer Roy E. Thurman   October 20, 1990

Officer Randal N. Young   August 28, 1991

Officer Bryant B. Bayne   July 21, 1995

Officer Tate D. Kahakai   July 21, 1995

Officer Dannygriggs Padayao   April 30, 2001